RANGER

MILITARY ILLUSTRATED
RANGER

BEHIND ENEMY LINES IN VIETNAM
WRITTEN BY RON FIELD

SERIES EDITOR: TIM NEWARK
COLOUR PLATES BY RICHARD HOOK

Current titles
Marine
Stormtrooper
Rifleman
Highlander
Ranger
SAS

Future titles
Paratrooper
Commando

**To all the LRRPs, LRPs, and Rangers
who served their country in Vietnam –
*Sua Sponte!***

First published in 2000 in Great Britain
by Publishing News Ltd

UK editorial office:
Military Illustrated, 39 Store Street,
London WC1E 7DB, Great Britain

Ron Field has asserted his moral right
to be identified as the author of this work.

ISBN 1-903040-04-3

Designed by Glenn Howard

Printed and bound in Singapore under
the supervision of M.R.M. Graphics Ltd,
Winslow, Buckinghamshire

CONTENTS

BIRTH OF THE RANGER

According to the Creed of the US Army Ranger, Genesis in the Bible is re-written as follows: 'In the beginning... God created the heavens and the earth. And the earth was without light, so God created light. And the light shined upon the greatest land mass, the United States. God saw that this was good. But in God's infinite wisdom, he saw that the United States would one day be jeopardised. So God created a protector, "The Ranger". And the light shined upon the Ranger. God saw that this was good. And on the seventh day, God rested. However... the Ranger remained awake.'

Ranger tactics and fighting methods were at the heart of the American frontiersman. From early colonial days, grim-faced men called 'Rangers' learned the craft of the Native American, and stalked his foe in the mountains, forests, and swamplands of North America. Although the era they lived in was much simpler than the present age, the skills necessary to become an *élite* soldier were the same. Often fighting in terrain that normal men shunned, the Ranger approached an enemy with the stealth of a slithering snake, and struck with the speed and lethality of a cobra. Lightly equipped and rapidly deployed, they waged war in the guerrilla-style of the Native American warrior and, in a sense, out-Indianed the Indian.

The first Rangers appeared on the American landscape in the 17th century, and were involved in some of the earliest disputes between the settlers and the indigenous population. In their original concept, Rangers were employed by the colonial governments to 'range' along the chain of frontier fortifications, thereby giving an early warning of hostile raids. During offensive operations they became scouts and trackers who located enemy positions for larger bodies of regular or militia troops. Their reports often included phrases such as 'ranged 10 miles along the ridge in pursuit of the foe'. Hence these men became known as 'Rangers' – and a legend was born.

RANGERS OF THE DEEP WOODS

The earliest known Rangers were formed during 'King Philip's War' in 1675, when the Wampanoag, a tribe occupying an area known today as Rhode Island, revolted against the enforcement of a treaty limiting their hunting and fishing rights. Led by Metacomet, or 'King Phillip', as he was known to the white man, the Wampanoag and their allies destroyed 12 townships and killed over a 1,000 colonists. In response, Captain Benjamin Church, of Massachusetts, formed a special full-time group consisting of friendly Indians and men chosen for their frontier skills. Church's Rangers, plus other independent ranger companies formed in their wake, carried out offensive strikes against the hostiles. Capturing Indian women and children, burning crops, and promising immunity to braves who deserted the cause, they finally managed to track down Metacomet to his swampy refuge near present-day Bristol, Rhode Island, on 12 August 1676. During a short struggle, the Indian chief was shot dead by one of Church's scouts. As a result, the Indians left southern New England, opening up the way for further European colonisation. The Rangers had won their first victory.

Other units did much to further strengthen the Ranger tradition as English settlers continued to struggle with the French, and their Native American allies, for control of the North American continent. Born at Barnstaple, Massachusetts, on 12 December, 1709, John Gorham was the original commander of the 'Indian Rangers of the Deep Woods'. As a young man he served aboard merchant ships and was occasionally involved in land speculation in Nova Scotia and Maine. Later, following the family tradition, he entered into military service in Massachusetts in 1741.

At the outbreak of 'King George's War' three years later, he organised a group of about 50 Rangers in New England who were sent to reinforce the garrison at Port Royal, Nova Scotia. Gorham's Rangers, composed of Mohican Indians and 'Border-landers', were later described by the French as 'destined to run into the woods... dressed in grey, cross pocket, with small leather caps or hats'. The unit conducted a highly successful free-ranging operation which employed tactics not commonly used by British regular soldiers, including raids and ambuscades.

Early in 1745, Gorham returned to Massachusetts to recruit additional Rangers, and was persuaded by Governor William Shirley to join the expedition against the French at Louisburg and Ile Royale. At the same time, he accepted a regular commission in the army of George II. Meanwhile, his Rangers were doubled in number and became part of the royal forces, receiving the same pay as regular troops. During the years 1747-48, Gorham's Rangers were the main defence of Nova Scotia, being supported by two armed sloops – the *Anson*, Captain John Beare, and the 70-ton *Warren*, Captain Jonathan Davies, both owned by John Gorham.

Following the peace treaty which concluded King George's War, the Rangers continued to play a vital

Rogers' Rangers during March 1758, as depicted by Frederic Remington. Discovered by enemy Indians as they travelled at night across the frozen waters of Lake George towards Fort Ticonderoga, they changed tactics and struck out overland in snowshoes by daylight.
Peter Newark's Military Pictures

role in furthering British interests in Nova Scotia. In 1748, Jean-Paul Mascarene, the Huguenot lieutenant-governor of Port Royal, ordered Gorham to subdue the French settlers along the disputed St John River. Following this, Gorham helped to establish Fort Sackville as a means of protecting the newly founded Halifax, and his Rangers were often involved in quelling disturbances among the Micmac and St John Indians.

Periodically, short-term Ranger units served under the command of John Gorham. According to the Boston *Weekly Newsletter* of 4 October 1750, 'Independent Companies of Rangers' were being recruited at the 'Sign of the Lamb' at the 'South End of Boston'. They were 'cloathed in blue Broadcloth, received Arms, Accoutrements, Provisions, and all other Things necessary for a Gentleman Ranger'. Included among these were Captain William Clapham's English Rangers, and a company commanded by Captain Francis Bartelo.

In 1749, John Gorham reached the apex of his career when he was appointed to the Nova Scotia Council. On 13 June, 1751, he launched the 10-gun brig *Osborne*, the first ship ever built at Halifax. In the meantime, trouble continued among the Native Americans, with Rangers matching the Micmac in brutality. On one occasion, 11 Rangers disappeared without a trace. On another, the Rangers brought in 25 scalps for bounty, some of which apparently had a blondish cast!

In 1751, John Gorham sailed for England on the *Osborne*, loaded with pine masts for the Royal Navy Yard at Portsmouth. Sometime in December of the same year he died of smallpox in London. His brother, Joseph Gorham, who had served under him as a lieutenant, succeeded to the captaincy of Gorham's Rangers and subsequently led them throughout the French and Indian War of 1754-1763. By 1756, the unit numbered 125 men, including five officers, one surgeon, four sergeants, four corporals, and two drummers. In lieu of a proper uniform, they were reported to be wearing 'French prize clothing', but by May 1759 they were described as having received 'a new uniform clothing, the ground is of black ratteen of frize, lapelled and cuffed in blue'. Two years later, five members of the company deserted from Fort Frederick. According to the Boston *Newsletter*, they wore red coats with brown facings, brown capes and waistcoats, 'linnen drawers; [and] leather jockey-caps, with oak leaf or branch painted on the left side'.

Gorham's Rangers went on to distinguish themselves in the French and Indian War, and in 1758 they played a decisive role in the capture of Louisbourg, the French fortress which guarded the entrance to the St Lawrence River. The next year they were one of six Ranger companies serving under General James Wolfe when he took Quebec. Obviously the most efficient of the Ranger leaders, Joseph Gorham, frequently appears to have functioned as a task force commander during the rest of the Canadian campaign. In 1761, his services were duly rewarded when he was commissioned a major in the regular British service. Around the same time, the men he commanded became known as the 'Corps of Rangers', or 'North American Rangers' – sometimes referred to as a regiment of light infantry.

During 1762, part or all of the Nova Scotia Ranger companies were involved in the expedition to capture Havana, Spain's chief naval station in the New World. After this, the much depleted Rangers were absorbed into various British regiments, while Gorham and his officers returned to America to recruit fresh volunteers. The company-size unit they raised was known as 'His Majesty's Corps of Rangers'. A Ranger sergeant who deserted at this time was described as wearing 'a red coat, waistcoat, and breeches, with silver vellum buttonholes'. Clearly, the late-war Rangers had adopted a uniform more in keeping with the regular British Army, although privates deserting at the same time appear to have worn civilian clothing.

Elements of this new unit, either serving with or drafted into the 17th Regiment of Foot, took part in the fighting around Detroit during Pontiac's Rebellion of 1763. By the end of the following year, the remnants of the original Gorham's Rangers had been disbanded. Although impoverished during his military service, and pressed on all sides by creditors after the war, Joseph Gorham was eventually rewarded in 1782 with the lieutenant governorship of Newfoundland.

The Gorham brothers left no known set of tactical instructions. Their actions, however, introduced a style of irregular warfare stressing mobility, surprise, and aggression. During the years 1744 to 1763, Gorham's Rangers served alternately as skilled woodsmen and as 'marine commandos', operating aboard the sloops of their original commander. They did more than any other military command to keep Nova Scotia English. The tactics originally developed by John Gorham were subsequently employed by others – particularly Robert Rogers, who earned even greater fame as a Ranger.

ROGERS' RANGERS

It was Rogers' Rangers who received much of the later credit for developing the Ranger way of war. Born at Methuen, Massachusetts, on 7 November 1731, Robert Rogers grew up in New Hampshire, where he learned the skills of the woods from Indians and hunters. Later becoming an articulate and persuasive military commander with a magnetic personality, he trained his men to 'Move fast and hit hard', thereby further setting the standard for future generations to follow. Operating in the days when leaders personally recruited their men, he wrote a 'Plan of Discipline' consisting of 28 rules emphasising operational readiness and aggressive tactics. His first rule required each man to parade every evening equipped with 'a firelock, 60 rounds of powder

and ball, and a hatchet... so as to be ready on any emergency at a minute's warning'. Less orthodox rules, in an age when parade ground tactics dictated battle performance, stated – 'If you are obliged to receive the enemy's fire, fall, or squat down, till it is over; then rise and discharge at them', and, 'when pushed upon by the enemy, reserve your fire till they approach very near, which will... give you an opportunity of rushing upon them with your hatchets and cutlasses to the better advantage.'

Rogers originally volunteered for service with the British army in 1755 to avoid punishment by the courts for counterfeiting. Based at Fort William Henry, a new post erected at the southern end of Lake George in New York colony, he quickly distinguished himself as a scout and Ranger. During March 1756, he was summoned to Boston by General William Shirley, commander-in-chief of British regular forces in North America. After a discussion of tactics, he was quickly appointed 'Captain of an Independent Company of Rangers to be furthwith [sic] raised' for employment 'in Obtaining Intelligence of the Strength, Situation and Motions of the Enemy as well as Other Services for which Rangers or Men Acquainted with the Woods only are fit.'

Several months later, Rogers was given command of three Ranging Companies, all of which were to wear 'A good hunting Coat, Vest, Breeches, a Shirt, a pair of Indian Stockings, Shoes and a Hatchet to be delivered [to] each man gratis at Albany – A firelock and Blanket to be Delivered Each Man at Boston, the firelock to be returned at the End of the Service'. By 1757, five additional Ranger companies, including one raised by his brother Richard, and another partially consisting of Native Americans, were added to Rogers' command. They were 'likewise to provide themselves with good warm clothing which must be uniform in every company... And the Company of Indians to be dressed in all respects in true Indian fashion'.

Units designated as
Rangers fought on both sides
during the Revolutionary War.
This painting by H.A. Ogden
depicts Ranger-style units
of the American Continental
Army between 1776-1779.
The man in the white hunting
shirt and trousers is a
member of Daniel Morgan's
'Corps of Rangers'. To his right
is a Rawlings Rifleman.
*Peter Newark's Military
Pictures*

An early success for Rogers' Rangers occurred on the eve of St. Patrick's Day, 1757. Although the remainder of the garrison at Fort William Henry were permitted to over-indulge in rum, First Lieutenant John Stark, commanding the Rangers in the absence of Robert Rogers, refused to permit his men to join in the celebrations. When the French predictably attacked that night, the Rangers were the only unit prepared to hold off the initial assault until the drunken soldiers could be rallied. Rogers' Rangers served at Fort William Henry until May, when they were ordered to Halifax to join in the expedition against Louisbourg. After the failure of this campaign, they were ordered to Fort Edward, which became the unit's headquarters for the remainder of the war.

ROGERS' SILENT MASSACRE

On 10 March 1758, Rogers received orders to march with 180 Rangers to the neighborhood of Fort Ticonderoga. Protesting that this force was too small, he asked to be allowed to take 400 men, but was refused. The march was made along the solid ice of the lake, moving by night and hiding during the day. Discovered by the enemy, who had been very active since the fall of Fort William Henry, Rogers changed tactics and led his men overland in snowshoes by daylight. Towards dusk, scouts brought word that a band of 96 Indians was approaching. On the left of the line of march was a stream, and on the right a mountain. The Rangers extended their line, and fired first, killing over 40 of the approaching warriors. Believing this to be the main enemy force, Rogers urged his men to press on in pursuit of the survivors, when suddenly they were attacked by over 600 Canadians and Indians. Falling back to their original position 'at the expense of 50 men killed', the Rangers held on for an hour until ordered to disperse with 'every man for himself'. Driven towards a precipice which dropped about 100 feet to a lake below, Rogers and a party of 20 men tumbled and slid into the water, and eventually made good their escape. Once word reached Fort Edward, a relief party was sent to their aid with sleighs and blankets.

The most memorable mission for Rogers' Rangers began on 13 September 1759. Major General Jeffrey Amherst ordered their commander to lead an expedition consisting of 200 picked men against the fierce Abenaki, part of the Algonquin group of tribes, who were camped near the St Lawrence River at St Francis, about 40 miles south of Montreal. Staunch allies of the French, the Abenaki had recently captured and beaten a British messenger carrying a flag of truce,

and were responsible for the death of over 600 colonists during the years of war. Rogers' command for this operation included a small platoon of the 80th Regiment of Light Infantry, a unit raised by General Thomas Gage, who wished to develop a Regular Army-style Ranger unit to emulate and eventually replace Rogers' Rangers. That night, as the moon rose over Crown Point on the western shore of Lake Champlain, the small band sailed out on their mission. Their task was to penetrate 300 miles into enemy territory through a land barren of provisions and occupied by a French and Indian army of about 15,000 men. They were to attack and destroy a powerful tribe of fierce warriors, and then effect a retreat through hostile country, pursued by a foe prepared to use any means to destroy them.

Even the trip up the lake was a dangerous one, as the French guarded the way to Canada with schooners armed with cannon. Once again, the Rangers travelled by night, resting in hiding during the light of day. On the fifth day of the expedition, a keg of gunpowder exploded in their camp, injuring a number of men who, together with some sick, were forced to return to Crown Point. The loss amounted to 44 men, or one fourth of Rogers' command. Pressing on, the Rangers arrived at Missisquoi Bay undetected on the 10th day. Here Rogers hid the boats for the return trip, leaving two trusted Indians to guard them. Two days later, these Indians arrived with the news that the French had discovered the boats, and were now in hot pursuit of the Rangers.

After a hasty council with his officers, Rogers decided to push on and complete the mission. If they travelled at speed, they could out-distance the enemy, strike at the Abenaki camp, and then make their way back via the Connecticut River. Lieutenant McMullen was dispatched to Crown Point to inform General Amherst of the disaster, and have him send relief and provisions to the mouth of the Ammonoosuck River, 'that being the way we should return, if we ever did return at all'.

For nine days the Rangers marched through a spruce bog where the land was low and swampy, the greater part being covered with water a foot deep. At night it was necessary to cut boughs to make a type of hammock in order to sleep above the water. The day before reaching their destination, the Rangers came upon the swift-flowing St Francis River. Placing the tallest men up stream and joining hands in a single file, the entire company passed the ford in safety. The only loss was a few muskets which were recovered by diving to the bottom of the river.

Towards evening on the 22nd day after

departing from Crown Point, one of Rogers' scouts climbed a tree and spied, three miles distant, the Abenaki village. Creeping closer, they discovered the unsuspecting warriors in the midst of a celebration, and decided to attack just before dawn. At last the dancing and rum took effect, and by three o'clock the last of the braves had stumbled to his bed. The Rangers made ready, and with a stealthy step, advanced to within a quarter mile of the village. Rogers called another halt, and the men lay down and waited. By five o'clock, he had made the final reconnaissance and found the entire settlement asleep. Orders were given for the men to drop their packs, and the command was divided into three columns. Prior to the attack, several men slithered down to the river bank, untied the Abenaki canoes and pushed them off.

With the first faint blush of dawn reddening the eastern skies, the Rangers moved rapidly forward through the village. Every sleeping brave had his throat slit, leaving the women and children sleeping. In this way, the deadly Rangers massacred almost two-thirds of the warriors before the alarm was given. But there was little time for the remaining Abenaki to reach for their weapons. Their only safety lay in flight across the river. But the Rangers had pushed the canoes of the disoriented warriors out into the current.

General Francis Marion invites a British officer to his swamp encampment to share a sweet potato dinner under a flag of truce. *Peter Newark's Military Pictures*

Five English captives were found and rescued, while the scalps of more than 600 whites hung from wigwam poles. Embers from the fires were scattered on the wigwams, and soon smoke and flames marked the death of the village. By seven o'clock, the Rangers had killed over 200 warriors, with the loss of but one of their own. Never again would the Abenaki be able to field an effective fighting force against the British.

The hardships of the Rangers' retreat far exceeded those of their advance. The way led through endless swampland and over barren mountain ranges. After eight days' travel, their supplies ran out, but they survived on roots and berries. Divided into small squads of eight to 10 men, several of these detachments were ambushed and badly mauled. Some of the fittest preferred to make their way back directly to Crown Point, while most of the survivors struggled on to the Ammonoosuck River rendezvous, 100 miles above a post called Number Four (now Charleston, New Hampshire).

Fires still smouldered as the first Ranger finally staggered upon the rendezvous point, but all signs of life, food, and supplies, had vanished. After waiting only two days, Lieutenant Stevens, in command of the supply mission, had departed two hours before the Rangers arrived. With most of his men exhausted and unable to move further, Rogers ordered Captain Ogden and a captive Indian boy to set out by raft for Number Four. Provisions finally reached the Rangers 10 days later. Their ordeal was over and their mission had been accomplished. Relief parties were sent out in search of stragglers. Slowly the haggard survivors were gathered in, but it was two months before the Rangers, now reduced to a mere 93 men, had recovered sufficiently to make their triumphant return to Crown Point.

Robert Rogers continued in service until the end of the war, receiving the French surrender of Quebec in 1760. During the following year he participated in the Cherokee War in North Carolina, but by 1765 was beset by financial problems and fled to England to avoid his debtors. There he wrote two rather inaccurate books and a play about his frontier exploits, but on the strength of this literary success, was able to secure a commission in the 60th Regiment of Foot (The Royal Americans). Posted back to the colonies, he was given command of Fort Michilimackinac, near Detroit in present-day Michigan, only to be arrested by General Gage on suspicion of mismanagement of funds and, ultimately, a trumped-up charge of treason. Tried and acquitted, he returned to England to face further financial difficulties which eventually led to a jail sentence in Newgate debtor's prison.

REVOLUTIONARY WAR RANGERS

When the American War of Independence broke out in 1775, Robert Rogers secured his freedom and once again crossed the Atlantic to offer his services to George Washington. A retired officer of the British service on half-pay with uncertain political leanings, he was regarded with suspicion by some colonists, and as an obvious enemy by others. Arrested by order of Congress, he escaped and began openly to espouse the British cause. He was subsequently commissioned by General Sir William Howe to raise a regiment of loyalists which eventually became known as the Queen's Rangers. Lacking the resolution of his youth, and by this time prone to alcoholism, Rogers was replaced in command in 1777 by John Graves Simcoe, a captain of the Grenadier Company of the 40th Foot, who turned the First Battalion, Queen's Rangers into one of the most successful loyalist units of the Revolutionary War. In their green coats faced with blue, they performed a valuable role as reconnaissance and outpost troops. They fought in the Pennsylvania campaign, the retreat to New York, and Benedict Arnold's raid on Richmond, Virginia, and were with Cornwallis when he surrendered at Yorktown.

The Second Battalion, Queen's Rangers, under James Rogers, Robert's younger brother, also saw considerable service scouting and recruiting along the frontiers of New York, Lake Champlain, and what later became known as Vermont. They participated in the capture of Fort Anne and Fort George, and were instrumental in a raid on Ballstown, New York, where they netted a number of 'rebel' prisoners. Another important role performed by a large number of officers and men of the Second Battalion was as spies. Disguised as civilians, they penetrated the camps of the Continental Army and gathered invaluable information on troop movements and battle plans.

After relinquishing command of the Queen's Rangers, Robert Rogers attempted to raise one more regiment, called the 'King's Rangers' but, by April 1778, had recruited but 40 volunteers and resigned in a 'cloud of ill repute'. His days as a soldier were over.

Other loyalist Ranger units which emerged during this period included a 'Corps of Rangers' raised by Lieutenant Colonel John Butler, and the King's Orange Rangers, led by William Bayard of Greenwich Village, New York. Butler's Rangers were recruited in 1777 and contained a high proportion of Indians. In their 'dark green coats faced with scarlet and lined with the same, a waist coat of green cloth, and buckskin Indian leggings reaching from the ankle to the waist', they conducted a series of very successful raids in the Mohawk Valley, Ohio, Pennsylvania and other areas. At Cherry Valley, on 10 November 1778, an Indian contingent of this unit disgraced themselves by murdering civilian men, women, and children after discovering they had been fighting against rebel soldiers previously captured and paroled. The King's Orange Rangers were often used as marines to protect British and loyalist shipping from the depredations of Congress privateers. Like many other Revolutionary War units, this regiment either used the term 'ranger' in their designation or were commonly called rangers, but did not serve in that capacity in the traditional sense.

Although George Washington depended mainly on the regular troops of the Continental Army to fight the British, several traditional American Ranger-style outfits were organised. On 14 June 1775, the Continental Congress resolved that 'six companies of expert riflemen be immediately raised in Pennsylvania, two in Maryland, and two in Virginia'. In 1777, this force of hardy frontiersmen provided the leadership and experience necessary to form, under Daniel Morgan, the organisation known as 'The Corps of Rangers'. Combining Ranger tactics with expert marksmanship, this unit fought in most of the major campaigns, and distinguished themselves at Freeman's Farm and Cowpens. Having been horse-whipped for striking an officer while serving as a teamster for the British army during the French and Indian War, Morgan had a personal revenge motive for leading his men so ferociously. Prior to the battle of Cowpens, he displayed the scars on his back to each of his Rangers and ordered them to 'Shoot for the epaulettes, boys!' Morgan's riflemen were so important in the defeat of John Burgoyne's army at Saratoga in 1777, that the British general remarked: 'the most famous corps of the Continental Army, all of them crack shots.'

Lesser-known American units included Knowlton's Rangers, a three-company outfit consisting of hand-picked volunteers from Connecticut and Massachusetts. Commanded by Lieutenant Colonel Thomas Knowlton, they came into being in New York City during the late summer of 1776, and were used for long-range patrols behind British lines and as a means of capturing prisoners for intelligence purposes. On 16 September of that year, the unit encircled enemy positions at Harlem Heights, New York, in order to attack from the rear. Discovered by the British during deployment, they came under heavy fire and lost many men killed, including their commander. Several months later the remnants of this corps fell into British hands when Fort Washington was captured. Whitcomb's Rangers were raised on the Lake Champlain frontier in 1776, and consisted mainly of men from New Hampshire. A two-company unit, they performed a valuable reconnaissance role within the Northern Department until disbanded in 1781.

THE SWAMP FOX

Although not normally recognised as a Ranger, the greatest American guerrilla fighter of the Revolutionary War was Francis Marion. Incredibly daring, his small band of partisan militia terrorised the entire British army in South Carolina for two years, striking with fantastic swiftness, and then vanishing ghost-like into the swamps. To chase him was futile, for the 'Swamp Fox' was too clever.

Born near Georgetown, South Carolina circa 1732, Marion was for years a peaceful farmer. When the Cherokee War broke out in 1759, he joined the militia and commenced his military career, learning the Indian technique of surprise attack and sudden disappearance, using the swamps and forests as cover.

At the beginning of the American Revolution, Marion served as an officer in the 2nd South Carolina Regiment, Continental Line, rising to the rank of lieutenant colonel. With the fall of Charleston in 1780, he was appointed brigadier general and given command of the Lower Brigade of the state militia. An eyewitness described his arrival at Lynch's Creek 'dressed in a close round bodied crimson jacket, of a coarse texture, and... leather cap, part of the uniform of the second regiment, with a silver crescent in front, inscribed with the words, "Liberty or Death". A rag-tag outfit clothed in 'homespun' and without proper equipment, Marion's small 'brigade' of about 150 men was ordered to pin white cockades to their hats to distinguish themselves from loyalist, or 'Tory', forces.

From the safety of hidden locations such as Snow's Island, Marion's force crept out to attack the surrounding British forts and supply lines, staging a series of hit-and-run raids in the face of overwhelming odds. Using Ranger-style tactics based on Robert Rogers' *Plan of Discipline*, Marion would rest his command during the day and march at night, often attacking at midnight. His scouts always rode ahead to prevent ambushes, while others hid in tree tops and signalled the approach of the enemy with shrill whistles. If a bridge had to be crossed near an enemy post, blankets were laid on the wooden planks to muffle the hooves of the horses. A campfire was never used twice and when planning a raid, Marion kept the target to himself until the last moment. According to William Dobein James, who served under him, his men were in the habit of watching his cook, and if they saw him unusually busy in preparing any of the frugal fare then in use, they knew an expedition was imminent.

Marion's strategy bewildered the British, who complained that the rebels did not keep to the rules of 'civilized warfare'. Eventually, British Colonel Bonastre Tarleton, who often chased Marion into the swamps, nicknamed him 'The Swamp Fox', declaring 'as for this damned old fox, the devil himself could not catch him.' The activity of Francis Marion, and other partisans, both as a guerrilla force and as auxiliaries at battles such as Georgetown and Eutaw Springs, kept the spirit of independence alive in South Carolina until a standing American army led by George Washington could return to confront the main British force of General Cornwallis at Yorktown, following which the American victory was complete.

The Ranger service was revived in 1812 with the outbreak of another war against Britain. By the end of that conflict, Congress had created 17 companies of Rangers commanded by 10 captains and 41 lieutenants, the senior officer being Captain Pierre Andre. The Act of 2 January, 1812, which authorised their formation, mentioned they were to serve on foot or mounted for the protection of the frontier, and were 'to arm and equip themselves and provide their own horses'. Mounted Rangers were allowed a compensation of $1.00 a day, which was a substantial sum at the time. These units were not prescribed a uniform, and generally wore homespun linen hunting shirts, jean linen trousers, felt hats and, being recruited on the frontier, were armed with their own rifles, hatchets and hunting knives.

A force composed of 160 Rangers and mounted infantry, under Captain A. H. Holmes of the 24th US Infantry, defeated a larger body of British light infantry 100 miles south of Detroit, on the De Trench River, on 4 March 1814. The British were cut down as they advanced in parade ground fashion towards the crouching American riflemen. Colonel Anthony Butler, who commanded US forces in Michigan territory, reported later: 'In killed, and wounded, and prisoners, the enemy lost about 80 – whilst on our part there were but four killed and four wounded.'

Two companies of Rangers, commanded by Captains Boyle and McGirt, were formed among the militia of Georgia and Tennessee to fight under General Andrew Jackson against the Seminole Indians of Florida in 1818. Attached to the 4th US Infantry, Boyle's Rangers conducted a water-borne reconnaissance up the Yellow River and overland to attack a Seminole camp at Choctawhatchy Bay. During two days of skirmishing, they killed seven hostiles and took 16 prisoners, fighting over ground which today is Eglin Air Base, home of the Florida Ranger Camp.

TEXAS RANGERS

From the earliest days of westward expansion, armed mounted men had 'ranged' the outer fringes of advancing settlers' farms and homesteads to protect them from hostile Indians and other enemies. When Indian attacks first threatened Stephen F. Austin and his American colony in the Mexican province of Texas in 1823, he called upon a ranging company for its protection, declaring he would 'employ 10 men… to act as rangers for the common defense'. As unpaid volunteers, these men returned to their families and land when no threat seemed evident.

A contemporary engraving of Texas Rangers, around 1840. Colonel John Coffee Hays commanded a regiment of Texas Rangers during the Mexican-American War, 1846-48. Hays' Rangers were so dreaded by the Mexicans that they became known as *los diablos Tejanos* – the 'Texas devils'. *Peter Newark's Military Pictures*

By 1835, the struggle for Texas independence was about to boil over, and a council of local government representatives created a 'Corps of Rangers' to continue the work begun earlier. A more organised force, these men were paid $1.25 a day, could elect their own officers, and furnished their own arms, mounts, and equipment. The following year, when Texas declared its independence from Mexico, some Rangers took part in the fighting, though most served as scouts for the Texian Revolutionary Army.

After independence in 1836, the debt-ridden government of the Republic of Texas soon found that Ranger companies were the least expensive

Captain Samuel J. Richardson raised the W. P. Lane Rangers, which became part of the 1st Texas Partisan Rangers, Company F of the 2nd Texas Cavalry in 1862. Although his wide-brimmed black slouch hat and plain shirt may be considered normal wear, his jaguar-skin trousers, with conchos down the side seams, and matching revolver holsters, were certainly not. *USAMHI/photo by Jim Enos*

way to protect the frontier from Indians and the threat of Mexican attacks into the Texan side of the Rio Grande. Hence the Texas Rangers were formed into regular squadrons in 1841, being described as wearing dragoon caps, and dragoon jackets fastened with buttons upon which was a single star and the word 'TEXAS'. The latter is probably a reference to the grey fatigue jackets prescribed for the Army of the Republic of Texas in 1839. During this era, well-known Rangers such as Ben McCulloch, John Coffee (Jack) Hays, and Samuel Walker first earned their reputations as frontier fighters.

With the final annexation of Texas into the Union, and the Mexican War of 1846-48, the contribution made by the Rangers as scouts gained them worldwide recognition. They were first used to reconnoitre the most practical route of the army of General Zachary Taylor in its march to Monterey. Advancing ahead of Taylor's army during September 1846, Ben McCulloch's 'strange-looking company', part of the Texas regiment raised by Colonel Jack Hays, was described as being mounted on 'on quick, tough horses' and dressed in 'leggings, trousers belted round the waist, coarse red or blue shirts, and either a buckskin cap or a soft felt hat'. Each carried 'a heavy rifle, a pouch of bullets, a large powderhorn and a Bowie knife, and some had Colt revolvers'. Colonel Hays had put Samuel Colt's bankrupt firearms business in Hartford, Connecticut, back on its feet in 1846 with an order for 1,000 six-shot revolvers – two for each of his 500 men.

Ahead of Taylor's advance, at Monterey, lay the fortified garrison of General Pedro de Ampudia, who was noted for his hatred of Texans. When the final American attack was launched, McCulloch's Texas Rangers, assisted by US Regular Infantry, led the way to victory. It was later asserted that this unit enjoyed 'more of the trust and confidence of the commanding general than any other volunteer company of the invading army'.

Towards the end of 1847, General Winfield Scott required additional cavalry to maintain communications with Vera Cruz once Mexico City had been captured. One of the units he secured was Hays' Texas Mounted Volunteers, which reached the Mexican capital on 7 December of that year. Observing the Texans *en route*, an American officer recorded: 'About the middle of November, five companies of Texas rangers [sic], under command of Colonel Jack Hays, arrived in Pueblo... certainly an odd set of fellows, and it seemed to be their aim to dress as outlandishly as possible. Bob-tailed coats and "long-tailed blues," low and high-crowned hats, some slouched and others Panama, with a sprinkling of black leather caps, constituted their uniforms, and a thorough coating of dust over all their huge beards, gave them a savage appearance.' Because of their effectiveness against Mexican guerrillas, Hays' command became known by the natives in the region as *los diablos Tejanos* – the Texas devils'.

Following the Mexican War, frontier protection in the South West became the responsibility of the US Army, and the emphasis of the Texas Rangers changed as they were transformed into a state militia and took on more of a peace-keeping role chasing outlaws and *banditti* until the outbreak of the Civil War.

GRAY GHOSTS OF THE CONFEDERACY

A Union officer, whose misfortune it had been to cross swords with the 8th Texas Cavalry during the Civil War, observed that 'the Texas Rangers are as quick as lightning. They ride like Arabs, shoot like archers at a mark, and fight like devils'. Although not 'rangers' in the truest sense, Terry's Texas Rangers were one of many units which adopted a 'Ranger' designation early in the Civil War. Organised during August/September 1861 by Benjamin F Terry, a wealthy sugar planter from Fort Bend County, and Thomas Lubbock, of Houston, Texas, this 'crack cavalry regiment' contained companies such as the Lone Star

Carl von Iwonski produced this oil painting of Terry's Texas Rangers from life in 1863 or 1864. Evidently 'off-duty', the men depicted ride at a carefree gallop as Ranger Sam Maverick, of Company G, holds his two-quart canteen joyfully aloft. Units like this helped to enhance the reputation of the Ranger during the Civil War.
Peter Newark's Military Pictures

John Singleton Mosby, the 'Gray Ghost' of the Confederacy, conducted countless raids on occupying forces and became the scourge of the Union Army in northern Virginia between 1863 and 1865. General Robert E. Lee, who was no friend of guerrilla warfare, at one time declared: 'Hurrah for Mosby! I wish I had a hundred like him.' *Peter Newark's Military Pictures*

Rangers, and the Mounted Rangers, and served most of the war east of the Mississippi River, leaving two-thirds of their number on the bloodiest battlefields of the conflict. In September 1861, the *Daily Picayune* of New Orleans reported Company K, the Tom Lubbock Rangers, as being 'all athletic, powerful men and dress[ed] fantastically in hunting shirts of different materials, with large boots worn on the outside, coming over the knee, the Mexican spurs attached. Some wore fancy Mexican pants trimmed down the side with little brass buttons, and silk sashes around their waists, others had the Confederate flag, worked in different colored leathers to represent it, on the legs of their boots.'

As the Southern states came under threat of invasion by Federal forces, so they responded by forming bands of partisan Rangers, a soldier-type more akin to their 18th century forefathers. The first attempt to raise partisan Ranger units occurred in Virginia during the summer of 1861. In May of that year, the Richmond *Dispatch* advised that guerrillas would be 'terribly harassing to an invading force' and that their borders should 'swarm in every direction... with riflemen and mounted rangers.' Consequently, units such as Caskie's Mounted Rangers, the Valley Rangers, and the Border Rangers were formed. One Independent Company of Rangers recruited at this time by Joseph T. Rosser consisted of 'returned Californians and Texas Rangers'. Applicants were advised that only 'superior horsemen and expert rifle-shots need apply'. As they operated without official sanction, most of these early Confederate Ranger units were quickly absorbed into regularly organised regiments. Rosser's Texas Rangers eventually became Company K of the 10th Virginia Cavalry, while Robert Caskie's Mounted Rangers were attached to General Henry A. Wise's Legion and served as scouts in the Kanawha Valley. Exceptions included a unit led by Elijah V. White, which remained independent and fought with the speed and ferocity of wild Indians, hence they came to be known as 'the Comanches'.

As the Confederate government remained reluctant to assume responsibility for armed bands over which it had little control, it fell to the state of Virginia to satisfy the increasing public demand for Guerrilla Companies. On 27 March 1862, the legislature authorised a minimum of 10 companies of Rangers to be created for operations within Federal-occupied counties of the state. Finally on 21 April, the Confederate Congress passed a Partisan Ranger Act authorising the formation of bands of partisan

Rangers, in companies, battalions and regiments. Familiar with every woodland nook and mountain trail in the locality, such men as John Hanson McNeill and John Singleton Mosby responded to the call and became expert at surprise attack and ambush, after which they melted away, often eluding much larger bodies of enemy troops.

Under the new law, guerrillas were paid the full value of any arms or ammunition they captured from the Union army and delivered to a designated Confederate quartermaster. Designed to attract recruits to the partisan service, this provision became such an attractive proposition that volunteers flooded to guerrilla outfits at the expense of the regular forces. By 12 September 1862, six regiments, nine battalions, and 24 companies of Partisan Rangers were active in Virginia and in Federal-held areas as far south as Florida. By the following year, many of these units had fallen into disrepute, being reported as operating like 'bands of licensed robbers' who cared little whether they attacked friend or foe. As a result, the Partisan Ranger Act was finally repealed on 17 February 1864, and most of the Rangers were transferred to 'the regular service'. Secretary of War James A. Seddon, however, permitted a few guerrilla units to remain in existence operating behind enemy lines. One such oufit was Mosby's Rangers, officially known as the 43rd Battalion, Virginia Cavalry

John Singleton Mosby, the 'Gray Ghost', was born at Edgemont in Powhatan County, Virginia, in 1833. A frail but volatile youth, he idolised Francis Marion, the original 'Swamp Fox', and was expelled from the University of Virginia in 1852 for shooting a fellow student after a 'disagreeable allegation'. While serving a short jail sentence, he studied law using books borrowed from his prosecuting attorney, and upon release set up his own law practice in Bristol, Virginia, on the Tennessee border.

When the Civil War broke out, Mosby enlisted as a private in the Washington Mounted Rifles, 1st Virginia Cavalry, and fought at First Manassas on 21 July 1861. Appointed regimental adjutant, he was relieved of duty when the 1st Virginia reorganised, but subsequently offered his services to General J. E. B. Stuart as an independent scout. During June 1862, he guided Stuart in his first 'ride' around McClellan's army in front of Richmond. Shortly after this, on the way to the Shenandoah Valley to offer his services to General Thomas Jackson, Mosby was captured and held at the Old Capitol Prison in Washington, D.C. While aboard a prison ship awaiting exchange, he noticed General Ambrose Burnside's army

Next page, in this painting by H.F.F. Phillippoteaux, Mosby's Rangers attack General Phil H. Sheridan's supply train at Berryville, Virginia, on 13 August 1864. One of his howitzers, supported by Company D under Captain Alfred Glasscock, occupies the hill to the left, while in the foreground Captain William Chapman, with the Second Squadron, leads the charge. Over 500 mules, 36 horses, 200 head of cattle, and 212 prisoners were captured, although Mosby overlooked a box thrown off one of the wagons which contained $112,000 worth of greenbacks to pay Sheridan's army. *Peter Newark's Military Pictures*

en route from North Carolina to reinforce Pope's unit around Manassas in northern Virginia. Upon release, he made straight for General Robert E. Lee and delivered his vital news. Lee quickly thereafter began his advance north, bound for the battlefields of Second Manassas and Sharpsburg.

In January 1863, Mosby was granted permission to organise a Partisan Ranger unit to protect the region around the Loudoun Valley of northern Virginia. A bold, audacious, and crafty guerrilla leader who spread terror among countless numbers of Federal soldiers, he began his operations using only 15 men detailed for duty from the 1st Virginia Cavalry. Soon scores of energetic young Southerners were attracted to the independent cavalry commander. As one of his men explained: 'There was a fascination in the life of a Ranger. The changing scenes, the wild adventure, and even the dangers themselves exerted a seductive influence.' Mounted on the finest thoroughbreds in Virginia, each man in Mosby's Rangers also furnished his own food, arms, and uniform. When not on active duty, he took refuge in the farm houses along the Blue Ridge and Bull Run Mountains. Mosby recalled: 'My men had no camps. If they had gone into camp they would soon have all been captured. They would scatter for safety and gather at my call like the Children of the *Mist*!'

In a flowing, crimson-lined cape, and using a whistle to signal his men to disperse, Mosby conducted a systematic series of raids against Union outposts, moving swiftly and secretly, and always operating at night. In fact, he was one of the first American commanders to treat darkness as a friend rather than a foe! By 17 January, his men had taken 22 prisoners, and had caused quite a stir in Washington. In response, English 'soldier of fortune' Colonel Percy Wyndham, colonel of the 1st New Jersey Cavalry and Union cavalry commander in the area, despatched large patrols to seek out the Confederate guerrillas. Unsuccessful in their endeavours, the Federal horsemen often returned to camp to find that Mosby's Rangers had paid a visit in their absence.

Mosby and Wyndham soon became involved in a personal feud, during which the Englishman accused the Virginian of being a 'common horse thief'. Determined to avenge this slur, Mosby conducted one of the most daring raids of his career. Intent on capturing Wyndham, he led 29 men into the rainy night of 8 March 1863, declaring: 'I shall mount the stars tonight or sink lower than plummet ever sounded!' Slipping through the Federal pickets, they arrived near Wyndham's headquarters at Fairfax Court House,

only to learn from a captured Union soldier that the Englishman had been summoned to Washington. Fortunately, they discovered from the same source that a much bigger catch, Brigadier General Edwin H. Stoughton, lay sleeping in a house nearby. Forcing his way silently at gun point into Stoughton's lodging place, Mosby found the general snoring loudly after a night of champagne and revelry. Approaching the bed, he uncovered the sleeping general and slapped him on the behind. According to Mosby: 'The brigadier rose from his pillow and in an authoritative tone inquired the meaning of this rude intrusion. He had not realized that we were not some of his staff. I leaned over and said to him: "General, did you ever hear of Mosby?" "Yes," he quickly answered, "have you caught him?" "No," I said, "I am Mosby – he has caught you!"'

On the same occasion, Mosby captured '2 captains, 30 other prisoners, together with arms, equipments, and 58 horses... without loss or injury.' On receipt of the bad news, President Abraham Lincoln placed the episode in perspective, remarking: 'Well, I'm am sorry for that. I can make new brigadier generals, but I can't make horses.' Mosby's reign of terror went on throughout 1863, and by late summer of the following year he had killed, wounded or captured 1,200 Union troops, and had taken more than 1,600 horses and mules, 230 head of cattle, and 85 wagons and military ambulances. So completely did he control the counties of Loudon and Fauquier in northern Virginia that a 1,177-square mile area there became known as 'Mosby's Confederacy'. So persistently did he destroy and disrupt the Ohio and Alexandria Railroad that Federal Secretary of War Edwin Stanton ordered every house within five miles of the tracks to be burned unless its occupants were 'known to be friendly'.

Regardless of these efforts, on the night of 14 October 1864, Mosby's men managed to loosen a rail on that track, and settled down to wait for the next scheduled train. Falling asleep, they were wakened by a terrific explosion and crash. Mosby recollected: 'We did not hear the train coming... the engine had run off the track, the boiler burst, and the air was filled with red-hot cinders and escaping steam. A good description of the scene can be found in Dante's *Inferno*.' When they departed, the Rangers took with them over $170,000 of payroll money meant for the Union Army. Mosby's men used some of this cash to buy their commander a thoroughbred called 'Coquette' which became his favourite horse.

Federal forces continued to pursue Mosby, and at one point surrounded a house where he was believed to be lodging. Searching the place, they found nothing and left empty-handed, after which Mosby climbed down out of a nearby tree in only his boots and 'long johns'.

Mosby's luck almost ran out on 21 December 1864. Twice before he been seriously wounded, but somehow managed to recover quickly. As sleet fell that cold winter's night, a 300-man enemy cavalry detachment surrounded a farmhouse in Fauquier County where Mosby was dining with friends. Seeing a slight figure dressed in gray move past a window, a Union corporal fired his revolver, and the bullet struck the 'Gray Ghost' in the abdomen. In great pain, Mosby had the presence of mind to tear off his Confederate colonel's coat and bundle it under a bureau. When the bluecoats kicked open the door, the wounded Ranger gave a drunken Federal major a false identity, and he was left to die in his own blood on the floor.

But once again Mosby made an amazing recovery, and was back in the saddle by March 1865. But by that time, the days of the Confederacy were numbered. Mosby conducted his last raid on the same day of Lee's surrender at Appomattox Court House on 9 April 1865. Nine days later he met with Union officers but refused to surrender his Rangers. Disappearing once again, he assembled his men for the last time on 21 April 1865, and announced: 'I disband your organization in preference to surrendering…. I part from you with a just pride in the fame of your achievements, and a grateful recollection of your generous kindness to myself. And now, at this moment of bidding you a final adieu, accept the assurance of my unchanging confidence and regard. Farewell!'

The 25 years following the close of the Civil War witnessed the end of the American frontier. They also marked the bloodiest chapter of conflict between the Native American and the white man. During this period, a small United States Regular Army conducted 24 operations officially recorded as wars, campaigns, or expeditions, and engaged in 938 separate combat actions, sustaining 919 deaths and 1,025 wounded. The need for the bluecoats to employ men who understood the Native American horse warrior, as well as the Great Plains, quickly became apparent, and army scouts versed in the skills of the Ranger soon rode at the head of regular troops. Men such as William 'Buffalo Bill' Cody, 'Texas' Jack Crawford, and Al Sieber earned much of their fame as scouts for the Army. Formal recognition of Indian scouts came in 1868 when Major George A. Forsyth was authorised to recruit a force of 50 volunteers who would take to the field using the tactics of the Indians. Their task was to track and, where possible, attack the enemy in their teepees. Forsyth's Scouts were short-lived. On 17 September 1868 they were ambushed by a band of over 1,000 Sioux, Cheyenne, and Arapahoes near the Arickaree

Frontier scouts used Ranger tactics during the Indian Wars following the Civil War. Captain Jack Crawford, the 'Poet Scout', was illiterate before the Civil War. Battle wounds put him in a Union hospital where a nurse taught him to read and write. Chief of scouts under General George Crook during the Little Big Horn campaign, it is said that he was riding to Custer's headquarters with dispatches when the 7th Cavalry was wiped out. *Peter Newark's Military Pictures*

fork of the Republican River. Withdrawing to an island in the river, they kept at bay the Indians under Roman Nose, the Southern Cheyenne chief, for four days before finally being rescued by black troopers of the 10th US Cavalry.

In addition to the continued threat of Indians on the western frontier and a resurgence of pillaging by Mexican bandits along the Rio Grande, a new and perhaps even greater threat appeared, particularly in Texas – that of lawless Texans. In 1874, the Texas state government sought to restore order by forming two groups of Rangers: the Special Force of Rangers and the Frontier Battalion. Under Captain Leander H. McNelly, the Special Force of Rangers moved into the Nueces Strip, situated between Corpus Christi and the Rio Grande River, to combat lawlessness in that region. Meanwhile, the Frontier Battalion, a force of some 450 Rangers commanded by Major John B. Jones, participated in over 15 Indian battles, and effectively neutralized

the once powerful Comanches and Kiowas. Perhaps more importantly, this group dealt with more than 3,000 Texas desperados, including bank robber Sam Bass and the notorious gunfighter John Wesley Hardin.

WORLD WAR TWO RANGERS

The American military concept of the Ranger slumbered for the next 60 years until 1942, when the United States found itself at war with Germany. On 26 May of that year, Brigadier General Lucian K. Truscott, the US Army representative to the Combined Operations Staff of British Admiral Mountbatten, submitted a proposal to General George C. Marshall recommending the immediate creation of 'an American unit along the lines of the British Commandos'. The War Department quickly sent a cable to Truscott and Major General Russell P. Hartle, commanding all Army Forces in Northern Ireland, authorising the activation of the 1st US Army Ranger Battalion. According to General Truscott, the name Ranger was chosen 'because the name Commandos rightfully belonged to the British, and we sought a name more typically American'. It was fitting, therefore, that the organization destined to be the first American ground force to fight Germans on the European continent should be called Rangers in compliment to those in American history who exemplified such high standards of courage, fighting ability, and determination.

After much deliberation, General Hartle decided that his own *aide-de-camp*, Captain William Orlando Darby, a 31-year old field artillery officer with amphibious training, was the ideal man to command the new unit. Promoted to major, Darby performed a near miracle by organising the unit within only a few weeks of receiving his challenging assignment. Thousands of applicants from the 1st Armored Division, the 34th Infantry Division, and V Corps troops in Northern Ireland, were interviewed at Carrickfergus by his hand-

Above, Brigadier General Lucian K. Truscott, founder of the U.S. Army Rangers during the Second World War. According to Truscott, the first American ground forces to fight with the Germans on the European continent should be called Rangers 'in compliment to those in American history who exemplified such high standards of courage, initiative, determination and ruggedness'.
Peter Newark's Military Pictures

Opposite, U.S. Army Rangers undergoing arduous battle training in preparation for the D-Day landings in Normandy during 1944.
Peter Newark's Military Pictures

picked officers. Of the 2,000 men who volunteered, only 700 were accepted. Rugged and realistic training with live ammunition was in store for the Rangers at the famed Commando Training Centre at Achnacarry Castle, Scotland. Coached, prodded and challenged by the battle-seasoned Commando instructors under Colonel Charles Vaughan, the Rangers learned the rudiments of Commando warfare, and completed the usual seven-week course in only 31 days. Five hundred and twenty men of the 700 that Darby brought with him to Achnacarry survived the Commando training with flying colours. One Ranger was killed and several wounded by live fire. On 19 June 1942, the first modern Ranger unit, the 1st Ranger Battalion, was officially activated.

These Rangers saw their first action when 44 enlisted men and five officers, under command of Captain Roy Murray, took part in the disastrous Dieppe Raid of 19 August 1942. Attached to the 2nd Canadian Division and Nos. 3 and 4 Commandos, they were the first American ground soldiers to see action against the Germans in occupied Europe. Six Rangers were killed, seven were captured, and all won the commendation and esteem of the British Commandos.

The 1st Ranger Battalion spearheaded the American landings in Algeria under General Dwight Eisenhower during November, 1942. Conducting a silent night assault on the port of Arzew, they silenced two gun batteries and opened the way for the 1st US Infantry Division to capture Oran. Later, during February 1943, the 1st Battalion conducted the first behind-the-lines Ranger night raid at Station de Sened in Tunisia, killing a large number of defenders and taking 10 prisoners with only one Ranger killed and 10 wounded.

On 31 March, 1943, the 1st Ranger Battalion led General Patton's drive to capture the heights of El Guettar with a 12-mile night march across mountainous terrain. Surprising the enemy positions from the rear, while 1st Infantry Division

units launched a frontal assault, they swooped down on the surprised Italians, cleared the Djebel el Ank Pass and captured 200 prisoners. For this action, the Battalion won its first Presidential Unit Citation, and Lieutenant Colonel Darby won his first Distinguished Service Cross. After Tunisia, the Ranger Force (Provisional) came into being on 19 April 1943, with the 3rd and 4th Ranger Battalions being activated and trained at Nemours, Algeria, using the original 1st Battalion as the cadre. The 2nd Battalion had already been established at Camp Forrest, Tennessee, on 1 April 1943, in preparation for the invasion of Nazi-occupied Europe. Needed for the assault on Sicily in April 1943, Major Herman Dammer was given command of the 3rd Battalion, Major Roy Murray led the 4th, while Darby became executive officer of the whole force, which came to be known as Darby's Rangers. This unit led the 7th Army invasion of Sicily in July 1943, landing at Gela and Licata and capturing 4,000 enemy soldiers in a single day.

On 9 September, 1943, the three units, by then re-designated Ranger Infantry Battalions,

Opposite, men of the 5th Ranger Battalion inspect the remains of a German bunker after their successful landings on Omaha Beach on 6 June 1944. The Ranger in the foreground wears a second pattern, herring bone twill field jacket, pattern 1943 trousers complete with cargo pockets, M1 helmet with camouflage netting, and holds an M1 carbine. *Peter Newark's Military Pictures*

Above, men of either the 2nd or 5th Ranger Battalion are packed shoulder to shoulder aboard a landing craft before embarking for the Normandy landings, 6 June 1944. Note the diamond shape patch painted on the back of the helmet of the man on the right. This was orange superimposed with the

battalion number in black. The man second from right has a rocket launcher, or bazooka, tied together with his M1 rifle. A few hours later these men were scaling the perpendicular cliffs of Point du Hoc, and capturing bunkers on Omaha Beach. *Imperial War Museum photo # EA 25357* were the first 5th Army troops to land near Salerno during the Allied invasion of Italy. Swiftly seizing the strategic heights on both sides of Chinuzi Pass, they fought off eight German counter-attacks, and won two Distinguished Unit Citations. During this action, William Darby commanded a force of over 10,000 troops. Besides his Rangers, he led elements of the 36th Division, several companies of the 82nd Airborne Division plus several artillery units. As a result of this success, the US 5th Army and the British 10th Corps were able to advance against Naples.

All three Ranger units later fought in the bitter winter mountain fighting near San Pietro, Venafro and Cassino, during which they took and defended ridges, mountains, and towns. After a short period of rest in the Naples area, during which they re-organised and recruited, the three Ranger Battalions, were reinforced with the 509th Parachute Battalion, the 83rd Chemical Mortar Battalion, and a company of the 36th Combat Engineers. The re-vitalised unit became known as the 6615th Ranger Force (Provisional) under the command of Darby, who was finally promoted to the rank of colonel. Just before dawn,

on 22 January 1944, his oufit spearheaded the surprise night landings at the port of Anzio. Capturing two gun batteries, they seized the city, and struck out to enlarge the beachhead – a classic Ranger operation.

On the night of 29 January, 1944, the 1st and 3rd Battalions moved off the beachhead and infiltrated about five miles behind the German lines, while the 4th Battalion fought to clear the road toward Cisterna, a key 3rd Army objective. Advancing along a flooded irrigation ditch on the valley floor, the 1st/3rd Rangers walked into one of the deadliest ambushes in the annals of US military history. The Germans had reinforced the night before, and artillery, tank and heavy machine gun fire was poured point blank into the Rangers. Darby, with the 4th Battalion, attempted to reach his beleaguered men, but was forced back, taking 50 per cent casualties and losing all his company commanders. Of the 767 Rangers of the 1st/3rd Battalions who advanced on Cisterna, only six returned. Among the dead was the 3rd Battalion C/O, Major Alvah Miller, while the 1st Battalion C/O, Major John Dobson, was badly wounded. As a result, the 6615th Ranger Force virtually ceased to exist as an operational unit, but their sacrifice was not entirely in vain, for later intelligence revealed that the Ranger-led attack on Cisterna had helped to wreck a planned German counter-attack, thus thwarting Hitler's attempt to push the Allies back into the sea.

RANGERS, LEAD THE WAY!

Other units proudly continued the Ranger tradition in the European theatre of operations. With the imminent departure of the 1st Ranger Battalion for North Africa, the 29th Provisional Ranger Battalion had been established on 20 December 1942 at Tidworth Barracks in England. Commanded by Major Randolph Millholland, and raised among volunteers from the 29th Infantry Division, this unit also completed Commando

Lieutenant Colonel James E. Rudder, C/O 2nd Ranger Battalion, Seventh US Army, accepts the thanks of General Jean de Lattre de Tassigny, commanding general of the First French Army, for the part his men played in the liberation of the Alsatian city of Colmar, east of the River Rhine, on 2 February 1945. The unit colour guard is seen in the background. *Imperial War Museum photo # KY 52247*

training plus an amphibious assault course at Bridge of Spean. In conjunction with No. 4 Commando, they took part in three small raids on the Norwegian coast, followed by an assault on a German radar station on Ile d'Ouessant, or Ushant Island, off the tip of Brittany. After destroying the station and killing over 20 of its personnel, they left as a 'calling card' a helmet and cartridge belt both clearly marked: 'Maj. R. Milholland, US Rangers'. This little-known outfit was disbanded on the arrival of the 2nd and 5th Rangers from the US on 15 October, 1943.

The 2nd Ranger Battalion was activated in April, 1943, and was subsequently commanded by Lieutenant Colonel James Earl Rudder, while the 5th Battalion sprang to life on 1 September of the same year, under Lieutenant Colonel Max F. Schneider, former executive officer of the 4th Ranger Battalion. Arriving in England on 21 November, the 2nd Battalion trained in preparation for D-Day, being joined by Schneider's men during May, 1944.

The 2nd Ranger Battalion carried out the most dangerous mission of the entire Omaha Beach landings in Normandy on 6 June 1944. Remarking on the assignment given to Rudder, General Bradley observed: 'Never has any commander been given a more desperate

In January 1944, British Brigadier General Orde C. Wingate, leader of the famed Chindits during the Burma campaign, provided the inspiration for the creation of the US 5307th Composite Unit (Provisional), dubbed 'Merrill's Marauders' after their commander Frank M. Merrill. Colonel Merrill is seen far left, while General Wingate is stood at centre. *Imperial War Museum photo # MH 7873*

mission!' Companies D, E, and F assaulted the perpendicular cliffs of Point du Hoc, which rise up 100 feet above sea level, under intense enemy fire, only to find their main objective, a battery of six 155mm mobile coastal guns, was not there. Of the 355 Rangers who took part, 197 were casualties. Eventually a platoon led by Sergeant Leonard G. Lomell located and destroyed the unguarded guns about one mile inland, hidden in an apple orchard and ready to wreak a devastating flanking fire on both Omaha and Utah Beaches. Considered a classic Ranger action, for two days and nights Rudder's men fought on without relief and held their position until the 5th Ranger

Battalion linked up with them.

The 5th Battalion, with companies A and B of the 2nd Battalion, had landed on the western end of Omaha Beach where elements of the 116th Regiment of the 29th Infantry Division were pinned down by murderous crossfire and mortars from the heights above. The situation was so critical there that General Omar Bradley was seriously considering redirecting reinforcements to other areas of the beachhead, when General Norman D. Cota, Assistant Division Commander of the 29th Division, gave the now famous order that has become the motto of the present day

The first US troops to fight in Burma, the 'mule skinners' of Merrill's Marauders clean their rifles and graze their mules, while their outfit pauses to receive supplies, mostly iron rations , dropped by the 10th US Air Force. Veterans of the jungle training bases of Trinidad, Guadalcanal, and New Georgia, the 'Marauders' arrived in India during October 1943, and three months later embarked on a 100-mile circling march to the rear of the Japanese army at Maingkwan, averaging 20 miles a day over some of the world's worst terrain, to clear the Japanese from the path of the new Ledo Road, the Allied lifeline to China. *Imperial War Museum photo # EA 21092*

75th Ranger Regiment: 'Rangers, Lead The Way!'

Responding to the situation, the 5th Battalion scrambled across the sea wall and barbed wire entanglements, and scaled the pillbox-rimmed heights under intense machine gun and mortar fire. Some of the first troops to breach Fortress Europe, the Rangers advanced four miles to the key town of Vierville, thus opening the breach for supporting troops. Meanwhile, C Company, 2nd Battalion, was forced by rough seas to land west of their objective. Suffering 50 per cent casualties, they still managed to scale a 90-foot cliff, using ropes and bayonets, to knock out a formidable enemy position that swept the beaches with deadly fire.

Later, the combined battalions played a key role in the attack on the German fortifications around Brest in the La Coquet Peninsular. Following this they went on to fight through the bitter Central Europe campaign of 1944/45. Under the leadership of Major George S. Williams, the 2nd Battalion were mainly involved in defensive operations during the German Ardennes offensive. Earning the Distinguished Unit Citation and the *Croix de Guerre*, this unit was finally deactivated at Camp Patrick Henry on 23 October 1945. Between 23-27 February 1945, the 5th Battalion performed the type of operation for which it had been created when it infiltrated behind German lines to establish a roadblock on the Irsch-Zerf road, a major German supply route. Beating off several heavy attacks, they suffered 90 per cent casualties, killed about 300 enemy soldiers and took 300 prisoners, before being relieved by elements of the 10th Armoured Division. Awarded two Distinguished Unit Citations and the *Croix de Guerre*, this outfit ended service on 2 October 1945 at Camp Miles Standish, Massachusetts.

ALAMO SCOUTS

Rangers and scouts also led the way in the Pacific War. Lieutenant General Walter Krueger, commanding the US 6th Army, recognised the need for reconnaissance and Ranger-type units for the planned invasion of the Philippines. Based on the success of the Amphibious Scouts, a small composite unit of US and Australian personnel responsible for several successful missions into New Britain, Krueger set up the Alamo Scouts Training Center (named after the Alamo Mission in his hometown of San Antonio, Texas) to train selected volunteers in 'reconnaissance and raider work'. The Center was formally set up on Fergusson Island, near Dutch New Guinea, on 12 August 1944, with Colonel Frederick W. Bradshaw in command. At this location, small teams of highly experienced volunteers were trained to operate behind enemy lines in order to conduct intelligence-gathering and tactical reconnaissance in advance of US 6th Army landing operations.

The training they received was rugged, realistic, and very demanding. Hand-to-hand combat, intense weapon instruction, physical exercise, map reading, and jungle survival dominated the course. Part of the training

Veiled by an early morning fog, with a mule-handler paused in the foreground, infantrymen of the Mars Task Force cross a river over a bamboo foot bridge, advancing south as the renewed Allied offensive pressed the Japanese back into central Burma during 1944.
Imperial War Museum photo # NYF 49535

involved the men swimming out from shore while a Thompson sub-machine gun sprayed bullets into the water – this taught them to duck beneath the water in order to avoid enemy fire. In another exercise, men jumped into the water in full uniform with their weapons and all their equipment, and swam to the far shore. A mock enemy headquarters in an abandoned village was used to train them in assault and raider tactics. Most importantly, they were taught to conduct deep reconnaissance, static surveillance, and restricted combat techniques.

A total of 10 field teams, comprised of one officer and five or six enlisted men, were subsequently involved in penetration operations which provided forward reconnaissance, critical intelligence and, in particular, tactical support for Lieutenant Colonel Henry A. Mucci's Sixth Ranger Battalion. The Scouts evolved from a simple reconnaissance unit to a sophisticated intelligence collection group additionally supplying and co-ordinating large-scale guerrilla operations on Leyte and Luzon. During their two years of operations, the Scouts accomplished over 106 successful penetrations deep behind enemy lines in the Admiralty Islands, New Guinea, Leyte, and Luzon. Although reconnaissance was their principal role, they were also involved in several combat actions plus three POW camp rescue operations. During their two years of service, the Alamo Scouts never lost a man killed or captured. As such, they are the forerunners of the Rangers of the Vietnam War, and of US Army Special Forces. De-activated in November 1945 in Kyoto, Japan, they were never reconstituted, but their ethos and tactics remained very much a part of the American military thinking.

The 6th Ranger Battalion, activated at Hollandia, New Guinea in September 1944, was another Krueger creation. Commanded by Colonel 'Hank' Mucci, this was the first American force to return to the Philippines with the mission of destroying coastal defence guns, radio and radar stations. Securing several islands guarding the entrance to Leyte Gulf, three days in advance of the main 6th Army Invasion Force, on 17-18 October 1944, they mopped up Japanese resistance and destroyed all enemy communications. This unit next took part in the Luzon invasion, plus several behind-the-lines patrols and small unit raids, which served to prime the Rangers for what is considered the greatest and most daring raid in American military history.

On 30 January 1944, C Company, supported by a platoon from F Company, 6th Ranger Battalion, plus two Alamo Scout teams, who provided critical intelligence and tactical support, penetrated 29 miles behind enemy lines and rescued 500 emaciated and sickly prisoners of war held at the Pangatian Camp near Cabanatuan. Survivors of Bataan and Corregidor, it was feared that these men might be moved or executed by the Japanese before they could be liberated. Assaulting the main gate at dusk, the Rangers killed most of the Japanese garrison and, aided by Filipino guerrillas, carried 512 prisoners back to friendly lines. Intelligence reports subsequently confirmed that the Japanese were planning to kill the prisoners as they withdrew toward Manila. General Douglas MacArthur later commented: 'No incident of this war has given me greater satisfaction than the Ranger rescue of these Americans.'

MERRILL'S MARAUDERS

The modern concept of the Long Range Patrol (LRP) was first developed by British forces in India during 1941. Known as the Chindits, after the dragon statues fronting Burmese temples, their task was to infiltrate by land and air behind Japanese lines. From February through June 1943, the raiding expedition commanded by British Brigadier General Orde C. Wingate sliced through north Burma, demolishing bridges, military installations, ammunition dumps and railroads. With increased pressure needed to push the enemy out of Burma and open up the land link with China, President Franklin D. Roosevelt issued a call for volunteers for 'A Dangerous and Hazardous Mission'. In response, 3,000 men with jungle experience volunteered from posts in the Caribbean, continental US and south-west Pacific. Formed in November 1943, this American 'long range penetration' unit, initially known as Galahad Force, was transported to India where it received further training from British LRP personnel. On 1 January 1944, it was re-designated the 5307th Composite Unit (Provisional) with Brigadier General Frank M. Merrill in command, and was divided into three battalions, each composed of two combat teams containing 400 men each. On arrival at Ningbyen, Burma, in February, the 5307th was dubbed 'Merrill's Marauders' by *Time* correspondent James Shepley, and another Ranger-style legend was born.

Merrill's Marauders walked over 1,000 miles through the extremely dense jungle in north-western Burma, carrying all their supplies and equipment on pack mules. Without the support of heavy artillery or tanks, they fought in five major and 30 minor engagements from the Hukawny Valley to the Irrawaddy River, and virtually destroyed the veteran Japanese 18th Infantry Division. Employing tactics that would have been familiar to Rogers' Rangers, they penetrated deep behind enemy lines and caused utter havoc among rear echelon troops. The unit achieved its greatest success in August 1944, when it captured the only all-weather airstrip in northern Burma, at Myitkyina. This cleared the way for the construction of the Ledo Road, which eventually connected the Indian railhead at Ledo with the Burma Road to China.

No other American unit except the 1st Marine Division, which took and held Guadalcanal for four months, had as much uninterrupted jungle fighting service as Merrill's Marauders. But the price paid for their success was high. From February through June 1944, their recorded losses totalled 424 men killed, wounded or missing in action, and 1,970 cases of malaria, amoebic dysentery, mite typhus fever, and psycho-neurosis. Unofficial figures were much higher. At the end of their

The legend of the Ranger lives on in this post-Vietnam War photograph. On a training exercise, this team leader, wearing the Army's Engineer Research Development Laboratories (ERDL) jungle fatigues and carrying a PRC-77 radio, raises a clenched fist to halt 'the men with painted faces'. *Peter Newark's Military Pictures*

campaign, all remaining Marauders still able to answer morning roll call were evacuated to hospitals suffering from tropical diseases, exhaustion, and malnutrition or, as the tags on their tattered uniforms stated, 'A.O.E' – 'accumulation of everything'.

On 10 August 1944, the 5307th was consolidated with the 475th Infantry and attached to the 5332nd Brigade as part of what became known as the Mars Task Force, a combined infantry and artillery unit. This outfit continued to push south from Myitkyina through the jungles to within 120 miles of Mandalay by mid-December 1944, thus hastening the defeat of remaining Japanese forces in Burma by February 1945. In 1954, the 475th Infantry was re-designated the 75th Infantry, from which the modern day 75th Ranger Regiment was formed.

RANGERS IN KOREA

Ranger battalions were disbanded at the end of the Second World War, but when hostilities broke out in Korea in 1950, their skills were needed once again. Two months after the North Koreans invaded South Korea, General J. Lawton Collins, US Army Chief of Staff, ordered the re-establishment of Marauder Companies, later designated Airborne Ranger Companies, and selected Colonel John Gibson Van Houten to head the Ranger training programme at Fort Benning, Georgia. Volunteers were required for 'extremely hazardous' duty and training lasted six weeks, with airborne skills included for the first time. The response was astounding, with as many as 5,000 experienced Regular Army Paratroopers volunteering from the 82nd Airborne Division. In addition to the Airborne Ranger companies, an 8th Army Ranger company was organised in Japan and was the first Ranger unit deployed in Korea.

Instead of operating as battalions, the Rangers in Korea were organized as companies assigned to an infantry division on the basis of one 112-man company per 18,000-man infantry division. Wherever possible, company commanders chose the men they were to lead, similar to the colonial days of Robert Rogers. Eighteen companies were raised, although only seven arrived in Korea in time to see action. The latter included the 2nd Ranger Infantry Company (Airborne), the only Department of the Army-authorised, all-black Ranger Unit in the history of the United States. The 1st Ranger Company arrived in Korea on 17 December 1950, where it was attached to the 2nd Infantry Division. It was followed several weeks later by the other companies.

Throughout the winter of 1950 and the spring of 1951, Rangers went into battle, performing 'out-front' missions such as scouting, patrolling, ambushes, and raids. They also spearheaded assaults, and were deployed as counter-attack troops to regain lost positions. Regarded as 'nomadic warriors', they were attached first to one regiment and then another. The 1st Company executed a daring night raid eight miles behind enemy

A fire team of the 3rd Ranger Company, 3rd Infantry Division, advance into close combat action behind two M26 Pershing tanks during the Korean War on 11 April 1951. *Peter Newark's Military Pictures*

lines in order to destroy an enemy command post, which was later identified as the Headquarters of the 12th North Korean Division. Caught by surprise and unaware of the small size of the American force, two North Korean regiments hastily withdrew from the area.

Attached to the 187th Airborne Regimental Combat Team, the 2nd and 4th Ranger Companies made a combat jump at Munsan-Ni on 23 March 1951 in order to cut off retreating North Korean forces. The 3rd Ranger Company, attached to the 3rd Infantry Division, had the motto 'Die, Bastard, Die!' and conducted raids across the Imjin River to establish the extent to which the numerous trench works were actually occupied by enemy troops. The 4th Company executed a daring over-water raid at the Hwachon Dam, while the 5th Ranger Company, fighting as an attachment to the 25th Infantry Division, gave good service during the Chinese 5th Phase offensive. Gathering up every soldier he could find, the Ranger company commander held the line with Ranger sergeants commanding line infantry units. The 8th Company was known as the 'Devils'. Attached to the 24th Infantry Division, a 33-man platoon from this unit fought a between-the-lines battle with two Chinese reconnaissance companies. Seventy Chinese were killed, but the Rangers suffered only two dead and three wounded, all of whom were brought back to friendly lines. According to Joseph Ulatoski, a Ranger company-grade officer in Korea and brigadier general in Vietnam: 'For the Ranger in Korea, fighting outnumbered and surrounded was routine'.

With the stabilisation of battle lines in Korea during July 1951, the Ranger companies were de-activated, with the last unit being stood down on 5 November of that year. The Rangers, however, were not to die out, as they had done so many times before. The Ranger Department was formed on 10 October 1951, with responsibility for training Ranger-qualified junior officers and NCOs, who would return to their units to pass on Ranger skills and tactics. The first Ranger class for individual candidates graduated on 1 March 1952. Such knowledge and experience would prove vital in the jungles of Vietnam 18 years later.

Following the Korean War, the US Army began to re-evaluate the need for Long Range Reconnaissance Patrol companies (LRRP). The general North Atlantic Treaty Organisation (NATO) Air-Land Battle plan required LRRP units to conduct deep penetration operations up to 150 kilometres behind advancing enemy forces, and to establish an intelligence collection system for the NATO army ground forces operating in defence. The British had already trained Special Air Service (SAS) personnel to operate in small independent reconnaissance groups. In support of this development, the first experimental US Army LRRP teams were successfully established in 1958, and eventually developed into the 3779th and 3780th LRRP companies, both of which were activated in West Germany and attached to the US 7th Army on 15 July 1961. Both companies were commanded by a major, and consisted of a headquarters platoon, two patrol platoons with eight four-man patrols per platoon, a communications platoon, and a transportation platoon. During May 1965, the 3779th was re-designated D Company (LRRP), 17th Infantry, while the 3780th was changed to C Company (LRRP), 58th Infantry. Moved back to the USA in 1968 as part of the agreed reduction of European-based US and Soviet forces that year, D Company went to Fort Benning, home of Ranger training since 1950, and C Company arrived at Fort Carson, Colorado. The next great military challenge for the Ranger was the Vietnam War.

RANGER WAY OF WAR

Unlike Rangers in earlier wars of the 20th century, who underwent training in the US or in friendly nations overseas, the LRPs and Rangers in Vietnam were activated, trained and fought in the theatre of war. In fact, their training was a combat mission. Having volunteered for assignment to a Ranger unit, they were not fully accepted as Rangers until they had passed the acid test on patrol. Only then would the 'cherry' or 'new meat' be accepted by his peers. Following this, he was allowed to put on the unofficial black beret and wear the red, white and black scroll insignia on his shirt sleeve.

Volunteers for the Long Range Reconnaissance Patrols, and the Rangers of the 75th Infantry (Airborne), came from infantry, artillery, engineers, signal, medical, military police, food service, parachute riggers and other Army units. They were joined by a few of their former adversaries, the Viet Cong and North Vietnamese Army soldiers, who became 'Kit Carson Scouts', and fought alongside the Rangers against their former units and comrades.

Brigadier General Robert C. Forbes, who commanded the 199th Light Infantry Brigade in 1967, recalled that volunteers for reconnaissance patrol work within the 71st Infantry (LRP) Detachment had to be 'alert, quick-thinking, innovative, team players, resourceful, intelligent, well trained in basic fundamentals of soldiering, excellent health, dexterous, brave, steady under stress, capable of operating in unfriendly environments over extended periods, physically strong, and have a desire for dangerous and challenging assignments'.

A GOOD RANGER

Veterans themselves have offered various suggestions regarding what made a good Ranger. Kregg Jorgenson of H Company, 75th Infantry, recollected: 'For the most part LRRPs were young, cocky, foolishly brave, occasionally arrogant, and individualistic... We were extremely effective and

little recognized.' According to Emmett Mulroney, K Company, it required 'a dedicated soldier to be a Ranger. Love of country, and faith in military decisions, and possibly a little Gung Ho!' William B. Bullen, also of K Company, agreed that the best Ranger recruit was a 'volunteer with balls, stamina, and a hell of a lot of team-oriented smarts'.

The Rangers, and their LRP predecessors, were never much concerned with bureaucracy. Hence very few statistics were kept regarding age, race, or background of those who volunteered for Ranger service. One of the few official references to their actual age appeared in an H Company newsletter dated 21 July 1969, in which it was reported: 'Colonel [R. M.] Shoemaker [1st Cavalry Division chief of staff,] later told the company commander that he hadn't realized how young the members of the company are; by their excellent accomplishments and professionalism he had expected much older men.' The average age of H Company was 20.2 years.

Ethnic or racial origins also made little difference to the Rangers – it was the man, not the colour, that counted. As men who shared the exhilaration and terror of combat, they forged a brotherhood which ran far deeper than skin colour. In general, Ranger ranks included a slightly higher proportion of Hispano-Americans, Native Americans, African-Americans, and Asian-Americans. Many Cuban-born Rangers had a more immediate sense of purpose in volunteering for LRP service. Having escaped to the US, they regarded Vietnam as an opportunity to fight the same enemy that had overrun their original island homeland in 1959. Native Americans were also attracted to Ranger service, albeit in smaller numbers. As the original colonial Rangers had developed their woodland skills in order to 'out-Indian' the Indian, it seemed quite fitting that in Vietnam they should volunteer for LRP operations to 'out-guerilla' the guerilla. Don Dupont of E Company remembered: 'We had an Indian on our team by the name of Reddoor who was the son of

a chief. Every time he got a body count, he had the company commander write to his father confirming the kill so he would be authorized another feather in his ceremonial war bonnet when he got home.'

Although statistically fewer than in other specialist units, African-Americans played an important role in the LRPs and Rangers. Regarding one of his team members, Daniel Pope of 'Charlie Rangers' remembered 'a black guy from Harlem in New York, who was my rear security. I felt good having "Deuce" along, he was all business. He'd grown up in a different kind of jungle, but the instincts were the same.'

Vietnamese, Japanese, Korean, Chinese and Hawaiian-Americans, were also very effective in the bush, as their appearance sometimes gave Ranger teams an advantage of seconds while Vietcong and NVA regulars decided whether a chance jungle contact was with friend or foe. Lou Bruchey, H Company, 75th Infantry, recalled:

Sergeant Daniel Pope, leader of Team 2-1, Charlie Rangers, on a visual reconnaissance (VR) flight of a planned area of operation south of Pleiku during early 1969. According to Sergeant Pope: 'More than anything else, the VR gave you a realistic first hand eyeball look at what you had planned from the map. It's hard to really know for sure what's there by looking at a map. For instance, does the LZ have elephant grass 15 feet tall that would prevent the chopper getting to the ground? After a while you developed a sixth sense about it. You could look at an AO from the air and almost pick out the most likely spots for the enemy to be and know how the terrain would be to travel through.' Co E (LRP) & Co C (Rngr) Assoc., Inc.

'We had one Ranger, Ted Yoshimura, who was Japanese-American and also carried an AK-47. On one of his patrols, a couple of "gooks" saw him in the jungle and thought he was one of them. To his amazement, they walked right up to him, smiling and talking to him in Vietnamese until he blasted them with his AK-47!'

According to Sergeant Yoshimura: 'When one of the guys mentioned that I could wear NVA gear to fool the enemy, I didn't take it as a derogatory remark. I just took it as a statement. After some thought on the matter, I realized that it was actually a good idea. We always tried to come up with different ways to beat the gooks at their own game. I never thought we were any better than the enemy was but I felt we were more cunning and we tried to do the things they least expected. As far as the term GOOK was concerned, I was never called that or any other similar reference to the name by anyone in the company. There was a certain respect for one another and I embraced that feeling. Besides, we all knew that person could literally save your life some day...'

As 'Kit Carson' scouts, many North Vietnamese and Viet Cong prisoners, or *Hoi Chanhs*, who had rallied to the South Vietnamese cause by responding to the *Chieu Hoi*, or 'Open Arms', anti-guerrilla programme, were also happy to collaborate with US forces, usually in return for a financial reward. Fluent in the language, they could gain valuable and timely intelligence from on-the-spot interrogation of local farmers or VC suspects.

RANGER TRAINING

On-the-job Ranger training was supplemented by army field and training manuals, such as the revised 1968 edition of the *Field Manual 31-18, Long-Range Reconnaissance Patrol Company*. However, beyond the company commander and operations sergeant, it was rare to find a LRP or Ranger who was familiar with such a lengthy tome. Used instead to a limited extent was the *Ranger Handbook*, published at Fort Benning in 1953. Known as the 'bible', this pocket-sized, one-inch thick work with a tan cover, served as an important guide for trainers. Its chapters dealt with essentials such as patrol planning and leadership, communications procedures, aerial supply, and demolition. Practical skills addressed in other sections included building rope bridges, conducting water crossings, tying knots for mountaineering, plus first aid and survival techniques. It also contained valuable checklists developed by veterans of many missions.

Typically, the *Ranger Handbook* was not an official document. Its lack of verbosity and direct 'Ranger way' of describing things was positively counter to normal army literature, but provided the best preparation for the Ranger in the field. In reality only a few copies of the handbook saw service. The skills involved in performing silent and dangerous missions behind enemy lines were either learned 'one to one' from experienced veterans in the training area, or were gained on patrol in an actual combat situation.

Staffed and trained initially by graduates of specialist centres such as the Ranger Training Command at Fort Benning, Georgia, the 101st Airborne Division Recondo School at Fort Campbell, Kentucky, and the Special Forces Recondo School at Nha Trang, the bulk of volunteers for LRP and Ranger service came from ordinary line commands, who were prepared to 'carry the fight to the enemy'. These men remained with their units through some of the most difficult patrol action in US military history, and frequently fought much larger enemy forces when compromised on their various missions.

The training camp used by E Company (LRP), 20th Infantry (Airborne), from which 'Charlie Rangers' evolved, was established in 1967. According to Ralph 'Skip' Resch, 2nd Platoon, the programme there consisted of 'Karate PT early in the morning for about a week from a Korean instructor. One day we were given Tracking Classes from a qualified instructor from the Army Tracking School,

learning to track like an Indian. We were the ones who built the rappelling tower, the company latrines, wash racks, placed 2,000 sand bags around each of the platoon billets at Camp Enari, Pleiku. In others words, we were the sharpening stone on the knife, perfecting the cutting edge that the later members of E Company, and eventually C Company Rangers, would earn their hard fought for reputation on.'

By March 1969, 'Charlie Rangers', 75th Infantry had constructed a basic and refresher training facility at Ahn Khe, where they conducted a three-week course for all non-recondo-graduates during April of that year. There, volunteers fresh from other units, veterans of a partial tour, or those returning for a second tour, received additional preparation before joining a team on patrol. Initial training was conducted under the supervision of the operations sergeant, while instructors came from the teams who were nearing the end of their tours and had the most experience. The company then used the course for

An H Company Ranger conducting an AO reconnaissance in December 1970.
Co E (LRP) & Co C (Rngr) Assoc., Inc./Ted Yoshimura

new volunteers before they applied for a place in the Recondo school at Nha Trang. Instruction emphasized physical conditioning, map reading, radio skills, advanced first aid, and patrol-related helicopter insertion and extraction techniques.

Special Forces-trained Don Ericson volunteered for service in 'Charlie Rangers' during September 1969, and recalled of his time: 'Our training started at 0500 the next morning and we had our tails run off. We ran three miles that first morning, just a warm-up for what was to come. After breakfast the classes began. Over the next two weeks we would undergo intense physical training, as well as study advanced radio procedure to include coded messages, advanced first aid to include giving morphine and serum albumin, map reading and night navigation, six-man team tactics, ambushes, area of responsibility of each member of the team. Every member of the team would be taught every other member's job so that if the team sustained casualties any man could take over any position. The stress in training was on teamwork; one man working alone could jeopardize the other five. We were being trained to fight North Vietnamese, Viet Cong style. Two could play that game, and we were beating them at it.'

Ranger veterans could apply for further training at the Reconnaissance Commando, or 'Recondo',

A pre-mission inventory at the H Company area at Phouc Vinh, about 30 miles north-west of Bien Hoa/Long Bien during January 1971. Team Leader Terry Wanish is stood on the right. Attached to his belt is a baseball grenade plus several 'Med Kit' pouches to carry M60 ammunition. The man at left is trying on rappelling gloves. Jungle boots and light-weight rucksacks surround them on the ground.
Ted Yoshimura

School operated by the Special Forces at the west end of Nha Trang airfield. Originally established to train replacements for Detachment B-52, which conducted reconnaissance missions for the Special Forces, the Recondo school offered a rigorous and highly competitive course which turned out an *élite*. According to Lou Bruchey, H Company: 'The Ranger School was brutal. The idea was to eliminate "quitters" as quickly as possible. Out of my original class of 43 infantrymen, only eight graduated. Most trainees dropped out after the first day or two because of the harassment and the punishing physical fitness training.' Training also took place at division-level reconnaissance schools throughout Vietnam, which implemented patrolling basics taught by the Army Ranger School and the MACV Recondo School.

RANGER ORGANISATION

The organisation of a Ranger company usually consisted of a headquarters section, an operations section, a communications section, and several patrol platoons. The headquarters section was composed of the company commander, an executive officer, a first sergeant, a company clerk, a supply sergeant and supply clerk, plus mess personnel. The operations section was usually composed of a operations sergeant, an intelligence sergeant, and an operations specialist. The communications section consisted of a section sergeant and field radio repairman, and three base radio stations which functioned as radio relays, codenamed X-rays.

Each patrol platoon was made up of a platoon leader, a platoon sergeant, and about seven patrol teams. Teams varied in size. The six-man Ranger team was standard, while a 12-man team was used for most combat patrols. As time went by and personnel were rotated out for a variety of reasons, it was not uncommon for a team to consist of five men or less and to be led by a Private First Class (PFC) rather than an NCO.

According to Emmett Mulroney, K Company: 'My team size ranged from three to five men, mostly four'. The leader of a smaller team might also carry and operate the radio. Some teams were reinforced with an indigenous guide, a sniper, or a North Vietnamese deserter called a 'Kit Carson Scout'. Teams could also be supplemented by specialists, such as engineers or pathfinders.

Also due to limited available resources it was not uncommon for a platoon to deploy with only three six-man 'recon' teams. This did not keep teams from completing any mission they were assigned. After training together as a team, the men were capable of handling each other's duties and positions regardless of rank. On some occasions two or more teams would be combined into a hunter-killer reaction force, prisoner snatch, or downed aircraft search/recovery unit (SAR).

A six-man team consisted of a team leader (TL), assistant team leader (ATL), senior scout observer, junior scout observer, senior radio-telephone operator (RTO), and junior radio-telephone operator. Team leaders were usually sergeants or specialists promotable to that rank. The main qualifications for a team leader was combat experience, good leadership qualities, strong reconnoitring skills, an ability to 'psyche the enemy out' during patrol infiltration and

The Rangers of H Company, 75th Infantry (Airborne), preparing for a mission at Phouc Vinh in November 1970. Al Rapp applies camouflage paint to Glen McCrary's face.
Glen McCrary

movement, and an element of luck in keeping fellow team members alive. The assistant team leader was always the next most-accomplished man, while the remainder of the team doubled as grenadiers, marksmen, and medical specialists. Ranger teams were made up of men from such diverse places as Peoria, Illinois; Atlanta, Georgia; Sacremento, California; Emporia, Kansas; Rocky Mount, North Carolina; and Syracuse, New York. It was the men themselves who made the team – where they came from was immaterial. Nicknames abounded and indicates the type of men who became Rangers. A roster of K Company includes 'Ratman', 'Festus', 'Captain Hook', 'Wop', 'Fat Albert', and 'Baby Huey'.

MISSION PREPARATION

Ranger missions usually consisted of locating the enemy bases and lines of communication; determining and reporting the strength, equipment, disposition and organisation of enemy troops; maintaining surveillance over suspected infiltration routes; locating targets and conducting tactical damage assessments for air strikes, artillery, and ground attack; placing and monitoring sensor devices on enemy posts; and providing information on possible landing zones for airmobile operations. Special missions included ambush, prisoner snatch,

Men of a 196th Light Infantry Brigade LRRP team take a break before setting out to patrol an area 15 miles northwest of Tay Ninh during March 1967.
John Burford

and platoon and company-size raids.

Ranger companies received their missions from Division G-2 (Intelligence), and were assigned to each mission in co-ordination with Division G-3 (Operations). The Ranger company Operations Officer received a data base read-out from the Order of Battle section of G-2 which contained all intelligence information available about the proposed area of interest (AOI) as reported by previous units in the location. He then designated the area on the map in which the team was to operate. In theory, the 'box' selected consisted of four grid squares of 1,000 metres each square, but in practice the area was usually dictated by terrain, with boundaries conforming more to mountain ridges or streams. The team leader was then briefed on the mission. Issuing the Warning Order to his team, he next took part in a visual reconnaissance (VR) flight to choose at least two insertion landing zones (LZs), plus a likely route of march and extraction LZ. They also flew the border/perimeter of the area. The VR flight ideally took place about 24 hours before the planned insertion, with the Operations NCO/Platoon Sergeant also aboard.

Meanwhile, the assistant team leader checked over weapons and gear, and drew from the supply sergeant any special equipment needed for the mission. On return to the helipad, the pilot, who would also fly the team in for the mission, co-ordinated the time of insertion, while the team leader went to Artillery Liaison at the Brigade Tactical Operations Centre (TOC) to see if artillery coverage was possible. Returning to the company area, he then produced and distributed three copies of an overlay of the AOI (one copy each for Company TOC, Brigade TOC, and Artillery Liaison), showing insertion LZ, possible route of march, escape and evade (E & E) rally point, and extraction LZ.

The division air cavalry squadron normally provided air support for each operation, otherwise aircraft would be supplied through Division G-3. The craft used for each air insertion normally consisted of a Bell UH1 Huey helicopter, affectionately known as a 'slick' because it carried no armament, accompanied by utility helicopters and AH1G gunships for the over-flight. The same type, plus a command and control ship, were used for both insertion and extraction.

Mission details were finalised once the VR flight had been completed, and the Ranger team would be briefed on their mission, and prepare for insertion. Weapons were test-fired to check they were operating properly and ammunition was inspected for cleanliness or defects. Rucksacks were fitted and refitted to make sure they were as comfortable as possible. Warren Gallion, 2nd Brigade LRRPs,

4th Infantry Division, remembered that his pack included 'medical supplies, grenades, smoke grenades, claymour [sic] mines, radio batteries, poncho and poncho liner, and food. I always wore an ammo belt or tied a bandoleer of ammo around my waist or chest. Just about every pocket in my fatigues had something in it. I carried maps and code books in the leg pocket of my fatigues. Signal mirror and pen flares in my shirt pocket. The one place I cheated on weight was water. Water was heavy and we were told not to drink the water in the streams without purification tablets. The purification tablets themselves made the water taste nasty to me. We could always find springs in the Central

A pre-mission briefing for a LRRP team of F Company, 58th Infantry, of the 1st Brigade, 101st Airborne in 1966. Note they are dressed in standard olive drab fatigues at this early stage in the war. Note the 101st Airborne divisional patch on the beret worn by the man on the right.
John Burford

Highlands during the rainy season, and I don't ever recall any ill effects from filling my canteens with pure mountain spring water.'

Tom Reed, 2nd Brigade LRPs, 4th Infantry Division, added: 'I wouldn't skimp on ammunition. If I had to cut down somewhere, it was in rations. I usually carried only one LRRP ration per day with one extra in case we were extended. When we started carrying two radios, I carried the spare and let my RTO carry the active radio. When I started carrying a radio I stopped carrying a claymour [sic]. I devised a system where I could cover our night location with three claymours using both the front and backblast.'

Any loose equipment was taped, while gear that might rub together or make noise was padded. Known as 'breaking tape' or 'taping up', Rangers tested its effectiveness by jumpng up and down to check for rattles or noise – and added more tape or repacked their rucksacks. Men could not carry letters, paperbacks, or any other form of reading matter beyond the Signal Operating Instructions (SOI). Emmett Mulroney, K Company, recalled: 'We carried out NO letters or anything with an address on it.' Indeed, the only form of identification borne was dog tags, which were worn around the neck or tied to the boot laces. Before final inspection by the team leader, camouflage was applied to firearms,

An insertion by Armoured Personnel Carrier (APC) and tanks. Note the insignia painted on the side of the vehicle nearest the camera, which indicates the Ranger team being inserted was K Company operating out of 'Firebase Blackhawk'.
Larry Flanagan

equipment, and to the Rangers themselves. Thin strips of olive-drab burlap, or tape, were bound around weapon fore-grips and butt-stocks. Any shiny or reflective metal was spot painted or covered with yet more tape. Greasepaint from camouflage sticks was applied to the face, hands, and other exposed skin areas. US Army-issue camouflage sticks came in tin tubes about three inches long, with a cap at either end to protect the two-colour stick. One end was black, which was used by most teams to tone down dominant facial features such as cheekbones, nose, and forehead. The green paint was applied to all areas in between until all exposed skin was covered.

John Rotundo described a 'Charlie Rangers' team preparing thus: 'At 0400 hours the team was awakened by the platoon sergeant as quietly as he could without waking the men from the other teams. Team 2-5 headed for the latrine and did their wake-up call and then applied camouflage to their faces and hands. Team 2-5 put its cammy on in war-paint style to look meaner. When that was accomplished they headed for the mess hall for some coffee and a candy bar. Rangers tried not to eat big breakfasts, because that tended to make them feel heavy and move slower than usual. After chow they moved back to the Second Platoon tent, where [Gary] Frye and Lepp [John Leppelman] adjusted cammy parachute headbands around their heads. The others wore boonie hats. They then loaded their gear into a small trailer behind the company jeep and piled in. The driver took them to the helipad to catch the slick that would take them on the first leg of their journey.'

According to Jim Zwiebel of K Company: 'Looking back and thinking about going out on a mission – at the time I only thought about the pre-mission briefing. You would normally be told if the AO was hot, but sometimes their info wasn't accurate. You just basically told yourself that there was always the potential of danger on all missions. After pulling as many missions as I did, 36 of them – you just never let your guard down. That was our big advantage, the element of surprise.' Emmett Mulroney recalled: 'As far as preparing for a mission I never really thought about anything except our objective of that mission. I was never afraid of going on any mission. The fact is I always looked forward to them. I guess I was Gung Ho.'

When all pre-mission preparations were done, many units had a last minute ritual before heading for the helipad, which involved having a team photograph taken for inclusion in the 'company records'.

Unfortunately, Ranger teams were often scrambled into action at short notice, and the 'recon' flight was made only a few hours before the insertion was to be performed. Emmett Mulroney remembered: 'Even though we were supposed to have 72 hours stand down between missions, we never ever got that long. The most was probably 48 hours, but many only had two hours.'

INSERTION

The method of insertion of a patrol team depended on the nature of the mission, the weather, the terrain, enemy deployment, and support available. Teams were mostly inserted by helicopter, or 'slick' as the Rangers called it, although they were sometimes deployed by foot, boat, vehicle, or 'stay behind', on which occasion they remained in the jungle after the

Ready to load out for a mission insertion, this team from L Company, 75th Infantry, approach a UH-1 Huey in the helicopter revetments. Two men are armed with CAR-15s, while the 'Kit Carson' scout in the lead carries a full-size M16A1. Note the metal 'Parachutist' badge and regimental crest pinned to his black beret.
John Burford

main ground force had been withdrawn. According to Larry Flanagan, of K Company: 'We were always inserted by helicopters, anywhere from five miles to as much as 35 or 40 miles out depending on our ability to maintain "commo". The tanks were only used for a very short time when our helicopters were used for something else. They only went out a mile or less, and were far from ideal for our type of stealthy mission.'

Prior to a helicopter insertion, the operations officer briefed the aircraft commander on details of the mission and whether the insertion was to be via touchdown, jump, ladder, or rappel. Warren Gallion, 2nd Brigade LRRPs, 4th Infantry Division, recalled: 'A LRRP team was most vulnerable when they were inserted. A single helicopter just flying in and dropping us off would alert the enemy to our location and presence. To give us a chance we would fly with an entourage of gunships and other helicopters. The gunships would start flying low and fast across the tree tops near our landing zone. If the gunships didn't draw fire our helicopter would drop into the LZ while the gunships continued to fly at tree top level to distract the enemy. The four of us would clear the helicopter as quickly as possible, so the helicopter could return to the air and not give away our location. We would disappear into the brush and the helicopters would soon disappear also. We would normally lie still and quiet for about an hour to see if the enemy would come to the LZ to check out the commotion.'

Daniel Pope of 'Charlie Rangers' remembered an insertion in 'VC Valley', south-southwest of Ahn Khe, during January 1969: 'The chopper began losing altitude rapidly, we were going in! I rotated my body, reached down and placed one foot on the skid. Gripping my camouflaged M-16 with the long slender noise suppressor tightly, I shifted my weight to the foot on the skid and rotated my upper body, weapon first, outside the chopper facing forward. We were going in parallel to the base of the mountains next to where the tree line met the open plain. We were actually landing on the open plain, visible to anyone within a 180-degree radius of us. It had to be an acceptable risk though, the only other LZ was a klick further up the mountain and we were saving it for the exfil. Before the chopper could settle in the waist-high elephant grass we were off and gone into the tree line. Just into the tree line we crossed a fairly large stream that ran along the base of the mountains. As we moved the RT established contact with our Xray and gave us a thumbs up. We moved another 50 metres and lay dog.'

Not every insertion was successful. Flying in near Kontum, in the Central Highlands on 10 June 1969, Warren Gallion, 2nd Brigade LRRPs, 4th Infantry Division, recollected: 'I was going through my mental check list as we approached the insertion LZ for our next mission. I was leaning back on my pack to put my arms through the straps when I realized the pilot was trying to get my attention. He was pointing in a very animated way toward the front windshield. I straightened up till I could see what had his attention. Someone had popped a red smoke grenade in the LZ where we planned to land. The enemy knew we popped smoke to show the helicopters where to land. I had heard that the enemy would pop smoke to lure a helicopter into a trap, but this was the first time I had seen it for myself. Since my team was the only friendlies within

The three photographs on this page of 'Killer Team 1-6', P Company (Ranger), 75th Infantry (Airborne), capture the mood prior to a mission in Quang-Tri Province on 21 December 1969.

Above, Roy Burke (left), Gary Sinclair (right), and David Barber (rear right) wait for take-off. Shortly after becoming airborne, their chopper came under heavy enemy fire and crashed, killing the crew and all of the team except for Larry Smith. *Robert Dowd, Sr.*

Larry Smith (left) and James
Howard Dean (rear right)
joke with the camera man.

Team Leader Thomas Dowd,
carrying an M-60 machine gun,
heads for the chopper pad.

miles and we were safe on the helicopter, the gunships had a field day shooting up the LZ as we watched from above. When the gunships had done their job we asked our pilot to give us a crack... So we made two quick passes. The first pass we each fired a full clip of ammo into the LZ and on the second pass we tossed our hand grenades... It was an exhilarating experience. The contact automatically aborted our mission.'

Whilst serving Task Force South in southernmost I Field Force territory between July 1969 and March 1970, 'Charlie Rangers' developed a helicopter-based 'stay-behind' infiltration technique. As one team was being extracted, another team already on the chopper would infiltrate at the same time on a 'stay behind' mission.

Insertion by foot was the most clandestine method of entering a reconnaissance zone, and was only conducted when an area of interest was near a friendly fire base. It also required that the Ranger company operations section liaised with friendly units to ensure the team passed through their own lines unscathed. Patrols being dropped via vehicle, such as Armoured Personnel Carriers (APCs) and tanks, also had to secure 'passage of lines'. The vehicles involved were often given overhead gunship support, and usually made false stops before and after the 'drop-off' in order to confuse possible enemy observers. Insertions via water through either surf or via river were similarly disguised by false landings, with the team exiting the boat as it neared the shore or beach.

Once inserted in a 'recon' zone, the team 'lay dog' just off the LZ while the radio man did a 'commo' check and relayed an 'Insertion Report' giving time, location, and whether the enemy situation was 'hot or cold'. At this stage, the quiet allowed the senses to notice everything. The sudden snap of bamboo, the jet-like whine of mosquitoes, the dive-bombing flies, and even butterflies alighting on the guns. Daniel Pope of 'Charlie Rangers': 'This is the moment when you become part of the environment, your senses

tuning to their ultimate level. Every shadow, shape, and movement is assessed as a possible threat. Your mind catalogs every sound of your surroundings to assess whether its ebb and flow and rhythm is normal. If the birds and insects don't return to their normal activities soon, you've probably got company. And there's the sixth sense you've gained from many, many hours in the jungle. You can feel the threat, long before you can physically identify it.'

Provided a radio link was established, the operation went ahead. Otherwise, in the words of the Ranger: 'No commo, no mission!' Situation reports (Sit-reps) were subsequently rendered at 0600, 0900, 1200, 1500, and 1800 hours, and hourly on a half-hour basis during hours of darkness. In the event of a team being beyond normal radio communications, this schedule would have varied being dependent on relay through aircraft. To maintain as much silence as possible, all night reports were initiated by the ROC, or radio relay, rather than by the team. The RTO could answer by 'breaking squelch', a technique developed by the Special Forces, which involved keying the handset in 15-minute spurts. The brief transmissions enabled aviators to follow the signals through their helicopter homing devices, thus enabling them to locate patrol positions within a few hundred yards. Questions could also be answered with one 'squelch' for 'yes', two for 'no', and three for 'ask again'.

'Spot reports' were necessary when a significant sighting or enemy contact was made. Information relayed always followed the acronymn SALUTE – size of enemy force; activity; location; unit or uniform description; time; equipment observed. In the event of a firefight, additional data would be sent on body count and weapons/equipment captured.

ON THE MOVE

The thick terrain encountered normally forced Ranger patrol teams to move in a file formation, with each man ordinarily between five and ten metres apart in order to maintain visual contact with one

Top, **each man had time for his own inner reflections once aboard the helicopter. This photo of a Charlie Rangers team member on his way out to a mission captures the mood of antici-pation as the aircraft heads towards the Landing Zone.** *Bottom*, **Steve Mantooth of Team 4-2, Charlie Rangers, on the helicopter skids ready for insertion.** *Co E (LRP) & Co C (Rngr) Assoc., Inc.*

another. In more open areas, the file could be changed to a cigar-shaped column formation. As the file moved ahead, a six-man team would have been arranged thus: the senior scout observer acted as the 'point man'. Responsible for front security, early warning of enemy presence, and maintaining a general compass bearing, he assumed command in the event of the team leader and assistant team leader becoming casualties.

According to Daniel Pope of C Company: 'More than once when I was walking point, without knowing why, the hair would suddenly stand up on the back of my neck and I would get that sinking feeling in the pit of my stomach that fear brings.

That's when you start slowly backing up because you know you're in danger, you've learned to trust your instincts, they're what keeps you alive.'

Of his point man, Don Ericson, C Company recalled: 'When we moved through the bush, I often glanced up toward Murph. He moved like a cat; if he broke a twig when he moved it was rare. On point, his eyes never strayed from his intended destination. He moved the team at an incredibly slow pace so as not to miss anything. Murphy's biggest lesson for me was to never, ever walk trails. Wherever we went, we broke bush; noisier than walking trails, but we'd never walk into an ambush or a base camp.'

The team leader of a six-man team was usually

Team members of a Ranger patrol jump from the skids of the insertion helicopter as the back-up UH-1 flies overhead. This was the most vulnerable time for a team as their aircraft hovered feet from the ground. Note the jungle vegetation is being flattened by the rotor blade action.
John Burford

second in the order of march, and depended on giving silent rather than verbal commands to the point man. Hand or arm signals conveyed simple orders, while a notepad was sometimes carried on which to write more complicated instructions. As a last resort, voice commands might be whispered. Urination was permitted by tinkling down twigs to avoid noise Coughing was not allowed. A muffled cough could alert the enemy, who on occasions might be within 10 feet of the team. Prior to his first patrol near Phan Thiet, 'Charlie Rangers' Don Ericson recalled being told by a veteran team member: 'I don't even want to hear you fart in the woods.'

The senior RTO came third in the order of march, and was responsible for maintaining communications with the company tactical operations centre (TOC) or a relay station. He was also responsible for guarding one flank, and maintained a pace count to help the team leader control the course of the patrol. Regarding communications with TOC, Ron Coon, 2nd Brigade LRRPs, 4th Infantry Division, recalled: 'We used an early form of the tiers system, giving our location from a reference point such as "down 3.7, west 1.2". Whole numbers were kilometres that would give anyone that knew the reference point a six-digit grid of our location. You could just as easily give an eight-digit grid using the same system. Enemy locations were usually given in the "clear", but not always. When in contact with the enemy, all grid co-ordinates were in the clear. We never did use the official "Signal Operating Instructions" as they were almost always compromised.'

The assistant team leader came next and monitored both the compass heading and pace count in order to maintain a constant awareness of the patrol's exact location. He sometimes packed an M60, and usually carried the team aid bag. The junior RTO came fifth in order of march and guarded the other flank. Known as the 'slack man', he was also responsible for alternate or back-up communications when designated by the team leader. Last came the junior scout observer, who walked 'drag'. His task was rear security and 'sanitizing' the team's route to ensure that nothing was left behind which might alert the enemy to the presence of the patrol. This included straightening branches, disguising scuff marks on tree bark and, where possible, covering up any other obvious signs of disturbance to the undergrowth. Don Ericson recalled: 'Walking rear security was one of the hardest positions to walk in the six-man procession. Rear security walked backward more often than forward. The slack man always covered rear security when he turned to walk forward.'

During extended missions, the team leader might alter the order of march, plus individual responsibilities, to ensure that his men remained vigilant and alert. 'One of the advantages of being a LRRP was the team decisions,' remembered Tom Reed, 2nd Brigade 'Lurps', 4th Infantry Division. 'If someone was uncomfortable, they could speak up and we would all stop and take a break.'

When open areas were encountered, such as defoliated jungle or natural clearings, roads, trails, or streams – a Ranger team would, wherever possible, go around the danger zone or wait until dark before crossing. If the area had to be negotiated during daylight, the point man would cross to the far side alone and 'recon', before signalling for the rest of the patrol to follow. A previously agreed rallying point on either side of the danger area would be chosen, in case the team engaged with the enemy and became temporarily separated.

When making short halts, the Ranger team formed a 'herringbone' formation with the point man facing forward, the rear security man facing behind, and the other team members watching in alternate directions along the file. For longer halts off enemy trails, by enemy tunnel complex entrances, or holding night positions, a level position was preferred, and a security wheel was formed with one man staying awake at all times. Claymore mines were usually spread in front – hopefully in the

Once on the ground, the team ran to the nearest tree line and 'lay dog'. Forming a small defensive ring, they waited while the radio man did a 'commo' check and relayed an Insertion Report, giving time, location, and whether there was signs of enemy in the area. Communication with company tactical operations centre (TOC) or a relay station were vital. In other words, 'no commo, no mission'.
Co E (LRP) & Co C (Rngr) Assoc., Inc.

direction of the enemy. According to Warren Gallion, 2nd Brigade LRRPs, 4th Infantry Division: 'At night we would lay our backpacks side by side on the ground. We would lay out a poncho... and then all four of us would lay side by side, shoulder to shoulder... The person on watch would set up in his sleeping position. A mere touch on the shoulder would silently wake each team member into action... . Elephant grass was one of our favourite night locations as a LRP. The grass would be from four to six feet high. We could walk into it and trample down an area large enough for us to sleep. The trampled grass made a nice mattress!'

Where the terrain or circumstances dictated, the team deployed in a linear formation within arm's reach of one another. Claymores were set out to provide 360-degree protection in any position occupied for more than a few minutes.

CONTACT

When visual or physical contact was made with the enemy, an Immediate Action Drill was put into effect by a signal from any member of the team. In the case of a chance encounter, the first man to spot the enemy froze and signalled for the rest of the patrol to do the same. The team remained motionless until the enemy had passed by. If they were spotted, they opened fire immediately. According to Lou Bruchey,

Members of a LRRP team of the 25th Infantry Division leap down from their helicopter and dash for the tree line after being inserted into enemy occupied territory north of Cu Chi during January 1967.
John Burford

Next page, **Every team member keeps his eyes on his area of responsibility while the team is on the move, with the 'point man' facing forward, the rear security man sweeping up behind , and the other team members watching in alternate directions along the file. In this photograph, a 25th Infantry Division LRRP team works on patrol movement training near the Cu Chi base camp.**
John Burford

H Company (Ranger), 75th Infantry: 'We realized that one enemy soldier with an automatic weapon could wipe out an entire Ranger team. Also, because we operated in a "free fire zone", anyone we ran into in the field, man or woman, was considered an enemy. Additionally, because of the dense jungle vegetation, virtually every contact was at extremely close quarters. Contacts were usually very quick and very violent with little quarter given on either side. For these reasons there were rarely any survivors of a Ranger ambush or contact.'

On one occasion, while preparing to take up a night time position, Warren Gallion, 2nd Brigade LRRPs, 4th Infantry Division, was placing a claymore mine when an NVA column appeared in sight:

'I'm not sure if I heard the words or just felt them "Sarge… Dinks" . I dropped to my knees and froze. Out of my left eye, I could see a column of men walking toward me. Not on the trail a few feet away, but in the jungle next to the trail with me. Out of my right eye, I could see my men. Two were watching the NVA soldiers and the third was hiding the small fire with his body. The poncho [laid across a bamboo overhang] was green, but at this moment it looked more like a neon sign saying "Look here". I felt totally naked as I realized I had not even carried my rifle with me to place the mine. I started calculating at what point would I give away my location by breaking and running for my rifle. We were clearly out numbered and there was little comfort in knowing that we could probably kill eight to 10 of them before they could kill four of us. The point man was less than 30 feet from me, when he suddenly turned and started walking down the hill toward the stream. The whole column… more than 20 soldiers filed past me. They were all carrying extremely large packs. Several of the soldiers had their rifles strapped to their packs. They looked tired and most of them seemed only to be watching for their next step. When the last soldier moved out of sight I ran back to the night location and got on the radio. I started directing artillery in the direction they were headed.'

Contact on 30 January 1970. Ranger Team Killer 1-5, P Company, remove the clothing, equipment, and weapons from one of four well-armed NVA they had ambushed and killed minutes before this photograph was taken by RTO Terry Roderick, who was wounded during the action.
Terry Roderick

If the mission required the taking of prisoners, or other reasons necessitated engagement, the team organised an ambush. On spotting the enemy, a team member indicated this and pointed out the direction of the enemy. The team leader then signalled the team into position, and waited while the enemy proceeded as far as possible into the kill zone. Lieutenant Chuck Babcock of the 'Indiana Rangers' instructed the men under his command: 'Don't initiate [contact] unless you know what you're getting into. Look at the lead men. If they were smoking and joking, blow them away. If alert with weapons at the ready, let them pass. They're probably the point for a bigger unit close behind.'

Although any ambush formation could be adopted, the linear approach was most often used. It was simple, quick, and easier to organise. At the given moment, the team leader opened fire to begin the ambush. In the case of both sides spotting each other simultaneously, the nearest team member opened fire and the rest of the patrol swiftly joined the attack. Prisoner snatching operations were quite rare for some Rangers. Lou Bruchey of the 'Airmobile Rangers', remembered: 'Although H Company had lots of contacts and a great many enemy kills, I can remember only one enemy POW ever taken by our unit and that was a Montagnard tribesman suspected of helping the Viet Cong during the Cambodian invasion.'

When the enemy was either taken prisoner or killed, their clothing was always searched thoroughly. Intelligence gathering was the prime role of the Ranger, and many valuable documents and papers could be found sewn inside the lining of uniforms. The bodies of the fallen foe were often stripped completely and clothing was brought back for inspection by intelligence analysts.

As an *élite* unit feared by both the Viet Cong and the North Vietnamese regular troops, some LRP and Ranger companies waged a psychological war by leaving behind a wooden nickel on the bodies of the enemy dead. Having the desired effect, this often forced VC and NVA elements to move in larger groups, which in turn presented inviting targets for artillery and air strikes.

By 1969, patrol leaders of the Airmobile Rangers, 75th Infantry, were being reminded via company bulletins 'to pick up wooden nickels prior to departing on patrol. When stripping the enemy dead, a wooden nickel will be placed on the body'. Lou Bruchey recalled: 'I can remember trying to put one in the mouth of a "gook" I killed. Trouble was, his face, mouth and teeth, were so shattered, I had a tough time getting it in his mouth, and I can still feel and hear the bones crunching as I stuffed it in. Man, what a memory! In retrospect, the practice may seem a little barbaric, but because we worked in very small teams of five or six men deep in enemy territory, there was very little room for errors or misjudgments and no room for compassion.'

Captain George A. Paccerelli of H Company recollected: 'The wooden nickels had started when we were still Company E (Long Range Patrol), 52nd Infantry. I had ordered 1,000 of them printed with the Indian-head on one side and the company's identification on the other. They would be used for many purposes such as calling cards, thank-you tokens for the helicopter crews who put us in and took us out, and most importantly, for the reason stated in the bulletin, to spread fear in the minds of the enemy. They must have been effective, our patrols ran into too many enemy recon elements who were looking for someone.'

Each platoon of 'Charlie Rangers' had a card printed, which some left on enemy bodies as a calling card to announce whose work it was. Others used them in a less ominous manner. According to Daniel Pope: 'If you met someone and wanted to stay in touch you could give them a card with some personal info on the back like you would a business card.'

By 1969, Ranger missions and patrols were so effective that the enemy had organised their own teams who used 'Counter Ranger Tactics' to hunt down and kill them. Bounties of $1,000 to $2,500

Right above, Charlie Rangers produced its own calling card, which was left behind on enemy dead. *Co E (LRP) & Co C (Rngr) Assoc., Inc.*

Right below, wooden nickels were placed on enemy dead by members of H Company, 75th Infantry (Airborne) after a successful contact. First supplied to E Company (LRP), 52nd Infantry, by Captain George Paccerelli in 1968, the nickels were part of the psychological war waged by the Rangers. *Ted Yoshimura*

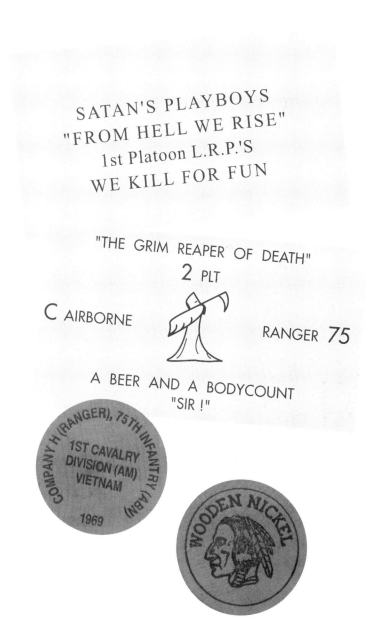

SATAN'S PLAYBOYS
"FROM HELL WE RISE"
1st Platoon L.R.P.'S
WE KILL FOR FUN

"THE GRIM REAPER OF DEATH"
2 PLT

C AIRBORNE

RANGER 75

A BEER AND A BODYCOUNT
"SIR !"

COMPANY H (RANGER), 75TH INFANTRY (ABN)
1ST CAVALRY DIVISION (AM) VIETNAM
1969

WOODEN NICKEL

were offered to these men by a country whose citizens were glad to do labour for 85 cents a day. Viet Cong and North Vietnamese Army veterans today admit that the 'men with painted faces' were the most deadly American unit in Vietnam. They were always showing up where they were not supposed to be, and usually when the enemy found out where they were, it was too late.

Main NVA/VC troop movements were greatly impacted by LRP and Ranger operations. According to a VC soldier captured by Team 1-6, 'Charlie Rangers' on 19 November of that year, enemy columns were preceded by a 'commo liaison man' who was completely familiar with all the trails, and served the same function as a 'point man' in Ranger teams. When nearing a likely ambush position, he led the following elements in a 'box' route which dissected the trail at intervals, rather than moving directly along it. In some cases the enemy 'boxed' the whole length of a trail if they thought that Rangers might be operating in the area.

Inevitably, some teams walked into an enemy ambush, and found themselves in the killing zone. In such a situation, it was not the Ranger team's mission to stand and fight. If an entire team were caught, withdrawal by fire was best accomplished by a 'leapfrog' method, during which one part of the team covered the other. Smoke or CS grenades were also very successfully employed to cover such a withdrawal. A team coming under mortar fire had to assume it had been spotted, and hit the ground on hearing incoming rounds. After impact, the team leader signalled a swift move at right angles to the original direction of march, in the hope of breaking contact. The same procedure was followed if hit by friendly artillery or mortar fire, while the RTO immediately called for an emergency 'check fire' on all radio networks.

EXTRACTION

Prior to extraction by helicopter, the company operations officer notified the team of the time it would take place, while the team leader delivered an 'PZ report' which included the type of extraction required; the location and size of the pick-up zone in metres; the height, type, and density of vegetation; and the degree and direction of any land slope. After delivery of this report, the team conducted a thorough 'recon' of the PZ to ensure it was secure, and reported their findings to TOC. As the command/control and lift helicopters neared the PZ, the team usually marked their location with a smoke grenade, and the lift pilot would confirm which colour smoke was in use before making his descent. In dense jungle, trees had to be blown up using C-4 explosives and claymore mines in order to create a 'hole' wide enough for a helicopter to land.

For a 'touchdown' extraction, the aircraft was set down in the PZ and the team boarded as rapidly as possible, after which the crew chief notified the pilot to lift off. A ladder extraction required the helicopter to hover above the PZ while the 'belly man' dropped the rope ladders. The team approached in threes, attached their packs to the bottom of their ladder with snap links, and scrambled up into the aircraft. Once the whole team was aboard, the helicopter ascended to a higher altitude where the ladders and packs were pulled inside. If a STABO rig extraction was required, two helicopters were needed as only three men could be lifted at a time. Once the men were in the rig, the belly man signalled and the helicopter made a vertical ascent until all personnel were clear of the trees. The second aircraft repeated the operation, and both machines flew to a friendly fire base with the Rangers suspended below. After making a slow vertical descent until the team reached the ground, the aircraft landed and the men climbed inside, and were flown back to company base.

In the case of a 'walk-out', the team followed a planned route of march in order to link up with friendly units. They then notified the TOC for further transportation. In an extraction involving either vehicle or boat, the team secured the pick-up position at the edge of the road or river, while the extraction unit proceeded to and beyond the pick-up point. As the transportation passed, the team made the appropriate signal. Upon verification of the team's position by the operations officer, the vehicle or boat turned around and headed back to the pick-up point where they stopped briefly to load the team aboard.

Emergency extractions were conducted when a team was in or anticipating enemy contact. These were usually carried out as per normal extraction procedures, except for emergency night time pick-ups via STABO rig and walk-outs. In the case of the former, the team used one strobe light to mark the PZ. A second strobe was turned on when the first load of three men was ready to be lifted out, and a third strobe was lit when the second group was prepared for lift off. Each group of three men kept a strobe lit when in flight to assist the helicopter pilot in lowering the team to the ground once in a secure area.

When no PZ was available, badly wounded Rangers could be extracted using a 'jungle penetrator'. Lowered by cable from a helicopter winch, this consisted of a three-foot metal projectile that unfolded like an anchor to form a seat in which wounded man, minus gear, would be hauled out.

During an emergency 'walk-out', the team followed a predesignated escape and evasion (E & E) route, while the team leader kept the operations officer well informed of the enemy situation, position, and strength. A team also performed an emergency 'walk-out' in the event that communications were lost and all efforts to contact the TOC, radio relay, or other friendly elements had failed.

Patrols were debriefed immediately on return to the company base. Debriefings were conducted by the company intelligence sergeant or by the unit commander, and usually took place in the company debriefing tent or similar location free from distraction. The written report included the time, location, and method of insertion and extraction; the route of movement taken by the team; the type of terrain encountered, including vegetation, height of tree canopy, trails, and water sources; the location, strength, activity, equipment, and weapons of the enemy; the results of enemy contact, including body count; map corrections; and the condition of the team members post-mission. Signed by the team leader and the debriefing official, copies of the report, plus appropriate maps and overlays, were filed under 'confidential' with the company intelligence section. Copies were also forwarded to division, and to other units operating in or near the area of interest.

A typical after-action report was that of G Company, 75th Infantry, who conducted a patrol from 0545 hours on 7 May to 1945 hours on 8 May, 1969: 'Two trails running North and South, well used. Three NVA, one with weapon, spotted. Three NVA spotted, carrying AKs and light machine gun. Two sighted, one with heavy pack. Seven spotted, two with heavy packs, five with weapons.' A lack of enemy sightings was just as important as actually finding the enemy, and often resulted in the safe movement of large ground forces through an area which otherwise may not have been penetrated.

After return to the unit base camp, a Ranger team neither rested nor cleaned up before weapons and equipment had been prepared for immediate deployment in case another team or a downed aircraft needed assistance. Once all had been prepared for an emergency, the men at last had time to attend to their personal care and comfort.

Member of a Charlie Rangers team using a signal marker panel to attract the attention of an over-flying Forward Air Control (FAC) pilot to locate team position. *Co E (LRP) & Co C (Rngr) Assoc., Inc.*

A Bell UH-D Dustoff Medevac helicopter of the 15th Medical Battalion, 1st Cavalry Division (Airmobile) hovers over the jungle canopy as the crewman lowers a jungle penetrator down to pick up a wounded man. The prongs of the penetrator folded down to act as a seat for the individual being lifted out. Both the helicopter and LRRP team were wide open to enemy attack during these medevac pick-up operations. *John Burford*

A wounded LRRP is hoisted on board a Dustoff helicopter via a jungle penetrator. Note the harness system which also helps him to retain his precarious seat hundreds of feet above the jungle. *John Burford*

RANGERS IN ACTION

The struggle which developed in Indo-China during the decade leading up to 1964 offered the Rangers the ultimate military challenge of the 20th century. Beginning as a determined attempt by the Viet Cong (VC), backed by Communist North Vietnam, to overthrow the Government of South Vietnam, the conflict widened into a limited international war as the United States and some 40 other nations supported the South with troops and munitions. Meanwhile, the USSR and the People's Republic of China backed North Vietnam and the Viet Cong.

Unlike conventional wars, the military struggle in Vietnam had no recognizable battle lines. Much of it consisted of hit-and-run attacks with the VC striking at scattered American outposts and disappearing into the jungle. In the early 1960s, North Vietnamese Regular Army troops began to infiltrate into South Vietnam to help the Viet Cong, and supplies sent to Hanoi from the USSR and China were carried south down the so-called Ho Chi Minh Trail.

The conflict escalated after North Vietnamese torpedo boats were reported to have attacked two US destroyers in the Gulf of Tonkin during August 1964. Acting on the resolution passed on 7 August by the US Senate, President Lyndon B. Johnson ordered a build-up of US Army strength in the Republic of South Vietnam and before the end of the year American combat strength there had increased to nearly 200,000 men. As each US Division and Brigade arrived in Vietnam, they realized the need for a long range reconnaissance patrol (LRRP) capability, and organized this to suit the needs of their command and the tactical area of responsibility. The LRRP units thus established were operational from May 1965 through December 1967, after which the Department of the Army authorised their reorganisation into the Long Range Patrol (LRP) companies of the 20th, 50th, 51st, 52nd, 58th Infantry, the 71st, 74th, 78th, and 79th Infantry Detachments, and Company D,

151st Infantry, Indiana National Guard. The word 'Reconnaissance' was dropped from their designation as these units began to perform not only reconnaissance-type missions but also combat operations such as ambush, prisoner snatch and raids. They continued to operate throughout the four military regions of the Republic of Vietnam, providing the major commands with much-needed intelligence to find the enemy and disrupt his line of communication and supply.

Conversion of the Long Range Patrol companies into the Ranger companies of the 75th Infantry (Airborne), finally began on 1 February 1969. The designation of the new regiment was very appropriate as the 75th Infantry was the successor to the 5307th Composite Unit (Merrill's Marauders), of Pacific War fame. Only D Company, also known as the 'Indiana Rangers', 151st Infantry, retained their unit identity and did not become a Ranger company in the newly formed regiment, as they returned to the control of the Indiana National Guard at the end of their tour of duty.

Although companies A and B of the 75th Infantry performed Ranger missions stateside for five years and eight months, and O Company was re-allocated to Alaska in 1970, some elements of companies C through I, K through N, and P, were active in Vietnam for a maximum of three years and seven months, from 1 February 1969 until 15 August 1972 – the longest sustained combat history for an American Ranger unit in more than 300 years of US Army Ranger history. During this period, the LRRPs, LRPs, and Rangers performed an invaluable duty as the eyes and ears of the US Army, and their many memories and stories reflect the courage and determination shown throughout countless thousands of patrols and missions.

CHARLIE RANGERS

The unit which evolved into C Company, or 'Charlie Rangers', 75th Infantry, was originally activated on

25 September 1967 as E Company (Long Range Patrol), 20th Infantry (Airborne), under the command of Major Danridge 'Mad Mike' Malone. Assigned to 'I Field Force Vietnam', they were formed in Phan Rang by recruiting combat veterans from the 1st Brigade (LRRP), 101st Airborne Division, along with personnel who were scheduled to join the Military Police Brigade. Additional men were also drawn from replacement detachments. E Company (LRP), 20th Infantry, was originally known as the 'Typhoon Patrollers', taken from the codeword 'Typhoon' used by I Field Force headquarters. At maximum strength, this unit consisted of 230 men, assigned to four platoons of seven six-man teams each. Each team was designated by platoon and team number within the platoon. Hence the first platoon, team 3 would be 'Team 1-3'.

On 15 October 1967, E Company was placed under operational control of the 4th Infantry Division, and was relocated to the Division's base camp at Camp Enari in western Pleiku Province. The 'Typhoon Patrollers' developed into one of the finest LRRP oufits in Vietnam during the course of the following year, co-operating with Special Forces-led native contingents of the 2nd Mobile Strike Force Command in Operation 'Bath' from March through April, and conducting over 400 patrols and missions.

With the re-constitution of the 75th Infantry on 1 February 1969, E Company (LRP), 20th Infantry, became C Company of the new Ranger regiment. As such, it was the largest Ranger company to serve in Vietnam. Maintaining its earlier reputation, this unit continued to serve under I Field Force at Ahn Khe, in Binh Dinh Province.

By April of that year, 'Charlie Rangers', under the command of Major Bill V. Holt, were pulling missions along the ambush-prone section of Highway 19 between that place and the notorious Mang Yang Pass. John Rotundo remembers the way these missions were reported from

Headquarters Platoon via loudspeakers rigged up in the company area: 'Ahn Khe proved it was a veritable shooting gallery from the first day the teams... were inserted. Almost immediately the loudspeakers were blasting away. First a siren sounded, then a voice called, "Attention in the company area, Team 1-1 in contact." Those of us in the rear area awaiting insertion or just milling around between missions cheered loudly.

'In a few minutes the loudspeaker gave us an update on the team's contact. "Team 1-1 reports engaging three dinks carrying weapons and rucksacks—gunships working area now", and again we whistled and cheered at the news. Fifteen minutes later the loudspeaker sounded the siren again then delivered another report: "Team 1-1 reports three confirmed kills, two AK-47s and equipment captured. No friendly casualties."'

HERE COME THE RUSSIANS!

At the end of January 1969, and on the eve of the creation of 'Charlie Rangers', a major NVA offensive was launched in the direction of Ahn Khe. Sergeant Daniel Pope found himself involved in a five-day surveillance mission to provide early warning of approaching enemy. Part of a mixed team of Rangers available at that time, he was inserted in 'VC Valley', south-southwest of Ahn Khe, to man a mountain top observation post.

Serving as assistant team leader, Pope recalled: 'For four days and nights we kept up a boring routine consisting of eating meals, watching the valley, calling in sitreps and pulling watch at night. The nights were so dark they were like ink. We had to move close enough together at night to pass the radio to the next man by touch because it was too dark to move. During the day the valley was beautiful and serene to look at, but remained empty. By the morning of the last day, the pressure was getting to us. I could tell by the way everyone kept to themselves except to perform their duties.

'We were set to be exfiled at 11:00 hrs that

Sergeant Daniel Pope, Team 2-1, Charlie Rangers, calling in a 'sitrep' from an observation post south of Pleiku in 1969.
Co E (LRP) & Co C (Rngr) Assoc., Inc.

Opposite, this atmospheric photograph of an H Company, 75th Infantry (Airborne) patrol crossing a stream captures the tension and heat of the jungle. The Ranger in the foreground with the M-16 is Bob Hughes.
Glen McCrary

morning, so I suggested to the TL that I do a little recon around the area to make sure everything was cool before we headed out to the LZ. The cherry [new guy] overheard me and asked the TL if he could go. I gave the TL a doubtful look, and he returned an "Oh, what the hell" one. I thought about it for a second, turned to the cherry, and said, "OK, you follow me, be quiet, and don't do anything unless I say so!" He agreed.

'We gathered up our web gear, checked our weapons and got ready to go. When he was ready, he nodded and I led us off the south side of the knoll. We headed slowly down the incline into the draw between us and the other finger that paralleled ours. We inclined up the opposing slope, picking our way through the tree trunks in a direction that would bring us to the tip of the finger.

'We had reached an elevation about equal to our OP when suddenly, I picked up movement in my peripheral vision to my left. I snapped my head to the left and found myself looking through an open tunnel in the foliage of the trees below to the plain on the other side of the stream. I moved my head sideways to scan the grass below, and then I saw him! A Caucasian, well over six feet tall, dressed in strange camouflage fatigues, without face paint, wearing a dark beret and without a weapon or pack. My mind snapped! It wouldn't accept what I was

LRRPs and Rangers spent a considerable amount of time in the water on patrol in certain areas of operation. Sometimes as many as three rivers would be crossed in a single day's march.
John Burford

looking at, but I knew it was real.

'My mind began to race, considering a myriad of possibilities. "Is it another LRP team in our AO by mistake? No, he'd certainly be carrying a weapon." Then, my heart stopped. An NVA came into view following three meters behind him, then another, and another. It was a point element!

'While I kept my eyes glued to the opening, I snapped my fingers to get the cherry's attention and frantically motioned him to me. When he got within reach, I grabbed him by the neck and thrust his face next to mine in front of the opening. The point element had passed and there was nothing there. I could tell he thought because he was a cherry, I was jerking his string. But then, more NVA came into view and I could feel him start to tremble as the adrenaline hit his veins. I whispered to him, "Get back and tell the team, I'm gonna get a head count. Move!"

'I watched in awe as the NVA filed past. I couldn't believe it, they were walking through the waist high elephant grass right out in the open, 20 metres away from the tree line, like they owned the damned place. They were force marching and really moving, they were in a hurry and they were moving straight toward Ahn Khe. Each one carried a large pack and was armed with an AK-47 or RPD machine gun. Every man was loaded to the max. There were mortar tubes, base plates and mortars, B-40 and RPG rocket launchers and rockets. There were large calibre crew-served automatic weapons and they were carrying 122mm rockets.

'The cherry was making a lot of noise. He crashed through the jungle like a mad bull, he was in a panic! I was suddenly struck with paranoia. If the NVA heard him we were in very deep shit, and I was separated from the team with 32 klicks to E&E. I glanced away for a second and saw him scrambling up the side of our knoll like his ass was on fire.

'Behind the point element had been a platoon-sized element, now none. Then another element. It was another platoon. I watched as they filed by in single file, aware of how much time was passing. The procession went on and I thought, "They're heading toward the knoll the team is on, what if the team makes contact. I need to get the hell out of here! No! I can't, I've gotta see how many there are." I was engaged in a battle of self-discipline.

'I was trembling from the adrenaline, my heart was racing, my breathing was becoming laboured from the rush and I was drenched in sweat. Four platoons had passed, with 20 metre breaks in between, and then there were no more. The count had been 210. I waited. Nothing. Satisfied, I broke for the team. I was moving as fast as possible without giving myself away when suddenly, it hit me. "Holy ssshhit! It was a Russian adviser!"

'As I crossed the draw I could see the TL climbing a tree at the tip of the knoll, exposing himself, to get a better vantage point. "Man, this guy has got balls!" By the time I reached the team, the TL was up the tree with the radio and spotter glasses. The team was frantically putting on their gear and getting ready to move. The NVA were headed into the stream bed below us for a break. As I hurriedly threw on my pack I could barely hear the TL giving a 105 artillery battery co-ordinates, "Negative Redleg, no spotter round, fire for effect between the co-ordinates and cover the blue line."

'He descended the tree and said, "I've already got choppers headed this way for the exfil and we got lucky, there's Cobras [Bell Huey Cobra, AH-1G attack helicopters] close by, they'll be here ASAP!" Before he could finish his statement we heard the distinctive sound of an incoming 105 round, then another, and another; then secondary explosions. The 105 rounds exploding and the accompanying secondary explosions, some of which were only 100 metres away, built to an incredible crescendo that was a deafening earthquake. By the time the barrage had ended we had counted 28 secondary explosions of various magnitudes.

'As the roar slowly subsided into an eerie stillness I heard the TL talking to the gunships. They were approaching our AO. He quickly briefed the spotter pilot who requested a flyby. I could hear the even drone of the little "loach" [Bell OH-6A Light Observation Helicopter] as he made a close pass parallel to the stream bed. "I didn't take any fire" he said, "I'm going in for a closer look." The pilot turned the loach and started a run at treetop level directly over the stream. We listened, expecting fire to erupt any second. "My God! I've never seen anything like this" he said, "there's bodies everywhere!"

'By this time, the radio was a buzz of activity. The slicks were inbound, ETA two mikes [minutes], and the TL was telling the gunships to cover our ass while we made for the LZ. The TL said, "OK, let's move!" We moved west off the knoll toward the LZ a half klick further up the slope. We moved as fast as we could, and the Cobra gunships started circling the area. The TL was talking to our 10 [Commanding Officer] and the slicks as we moved. I heard one of the Cobras roll and descend toward us head on. Suddenly, he fired rockets that came screaming over our heads so close I thought I could touch them. They exploded right behind us. "Check fire, check fire" the TL screamed, "that's us!" "Negative" said the pilot, "you've got bad guys right on your ass!" Deuce said, "I don't see anybody." The

Map of Republic of South Vietnam, 1966-1972, showing main LRP and Ranger areas of operation.

TL said, "Haul ass, move, move!" We did, glancing over our shoulder the whole time while the Cobras worked the area over.

'It seems like we made it to the LZ in seconds. Adrenaline can almost turn you into Superman! The slick, who was circling close, was on the ground before we could reach the centre of the LZ. The team ran for the chopper as hard as it could and dove onto the floor in a big pile, yelling "Go, go, go, go, go!" As the chopper blades gulped air, straining for altitude, I looked out at the smoke rising out of the stream bed and thought, "Son of a bitch… we did them a real number!"

'On arriving at our chopper pad in Ahn Khe, we found a jeep waiting with instructions for the TL and I to go with the driver. We were taken to the main Tactical Operations Centre where we were personally debriefed by the commander of the 173rd Airborne Brigade [Brigadier General John W. Barnes]. When we had finished briefing him, he said with genuine sincerity, "Gentlemen thank you, that's a job well done." Then he reached across the map table and shook my grimy painted hand.'

On 24 May 1970, Charlie Rangers were released from 4th Infantry Division control, having logged 30 patrol observations of enemy personnel, killed five NVA, and captured 15 enemy weapons. Four days later they were rushed to Dalat in anticipation of an NVA thrust toward that city. Numerous reconnaissance missions produced only seven sightings, but an enemy cache was discovered containing 2,350 pounds of hospital supplies, and 50 pounds of equipment.

The monsoon season began while C Company were at Dalat. Don Ericson recalled: 'Till then we had been used to 100-degree-plus temperatures; suddenly it was dropping to 70 or 80 degrees and we were all freezing. It rained every day and then the fog would roll through. Fog that dense would be trouble if a team had a heavy contact and the Cobras and gunship Hueys couldn't support them. Teams had already been inserted to probe the area. After a few weeks, minor kills were coming in but nothing major.

'About three weeks after we set up on a rare sunny day, all hell broke loose on the other end of the base's perimeter. Small arms and automatic weapon fire could be heard everywhere. The VC were attacking the general's golf course! Hard to believe the United States Government put a golf course in a combat zone. We had heard stories of bowling alleys and swimming pools around Saigon but had never seen them. Yet here was a golf course, and the VC were running all over it. And we were to be the reaction force. I could just see it; my parents would be notified that I died on the ninth-hole green defending some asshole general's golf course!'

INDIANA RANGERS

The only US Army National Guard infantry unit to serve in Vietnam was D Company (Long Range Patrol) of the 151st Infantry. In acknowledgement of their volunteer status, and to maintain their National Guard integrity, the US Army agreed not to infuse the unit with outside personnel. As part of 12,234 National Guardsmen called into Federal service from 17 states on 13 May 1968, the men who formed 'Indiana Rangers' hailed primarily from Evansville, Greenfield, and Indianapolis, in the state of Indiana. After extensive training at the Ranger School at Fort Benning and the Army School of the Americas in the Panama Zone, they arrived in Vietnam during December under Captain Robert E. Hemsel. Following further intensive training at Long Binh, they were declared operationally ready on 23 January 1969.

With the organisation of the 75th Infantry on 1 February, Captain Hemsell reported: 'We're ready to get to work. We've been training long and hard and morale is high.' Nonetheless, General Creighton Abrams, commander of Military Assistance Command Vietnam (MACV), had reservations about putting National Guardsmen in the field, and insisted on placing them under the overall command of Regular Army officer Major George W. Heckman, with Captain Hemsel as his executive. Despite earlier guarantees, the unit was also to be supplemented with Regular Army infantrymen as the Guardsmen voluntarily transferred out or became incapacitated. Once the latter had dropped below 50 per cent, D Company was to come fully under MACV control.

Despite these setbacks, the Indiana Rangers finally went into action on 8 February 1969. During its first six months' service, the unit conducted 573 patrols in southern War Zone D and eastern Bien Hoa Province, where it mainly engaged with the Viet Cong 'Dong Nai' Regiment. Patrols reported 134 separate enemy sightings and became involved in 94 combat situations, during which they claimed 76 NVA/VC kills, plus numerous other casualties via artillery fire and tactical air strikes. Before demobilization in November 1969, unit members were awarded a total of 510 medals for valour and service in the field.

The Indiana Rangers called their patrols 'baseball games' because they felt that individual team members worked together like 'the fingers of an outfielder's mitt'. On 28 February 1969, a 'baseball game' patrol became embroiled in a fierce firefight with a large VC force north-west of Bien Hoa. The team suffered three wounded and radioed for emergency medical extraction. The Air Force 38th Aerospace Rescue and Recovery Squadron's 'Detachment 6' despatched to the battle scene a chopper with para-rescue technician Master Sergeant David D. Rhody aboard. Riddled by enemy gunfire, the HH-43 Pedro helicopter was forced to return to base empty-handed. Undeterred, Master Sergeant Rhody volunteered to fly out in another HH-43 Pedro, while an Army Cobra gunship suppressed enemy fire sufficiently to enable a quick reaction force of eight Rangers to land and form a 40-yard perimeter around the wounded men.

Hovering overhead, the Pedro helicopter lowered Rhody to the ground, and he hoisted up two litter patients. As enemy automatic weapon fire increased, he waved the aircraft off and remained with the isolated team, providing life-saving medical treatment for the third wounded man. Another rescue chopper returned and, although holed by five enemy bullets, managed to pick up the beleaguered technician and remaining casualty. All three Rangers survived their ordeal and Sergeant Rhody received the Silver Star for bravery.

ELEPHANT PATROL

One of the most bizarre incidents in Vietnam War Ranger service occurred in April 1969 when an overnight patrol position in the jungle of Long Khanh Province was overrun by an elephant. At about 1800 hours, Specialist 4th Class (Sp4) Loren Dixon was observing the team perimeter when he noticed a large grey mass in the underbrush about 25 feet away. Suddenly an elephant pushed into full view and charged full-speed at the horrified Rangers. Screaming 'Elephant', Dixon watched as the great beast headed straight at Lieutenant Eric T. Ellis and Sp4 H. C. Cross, who dived to either side and emptied their 20-round M16 magazines into it. The enraged elephant next charged at Sp4 Ken Bucy, and grabbed him with her trunk as he tried to scramble away. According to Lieutenant Ellis, 'She had him coiled in her trunk and lifted him way up over her head. Then she flung him to the ground and lifted her foot right above his head when we opened up with the sixteens and a machine gun.' As the wounded beast sagged to its knees, a baby elephant dashed from the other side of the camp and the huge female groped to her feet and disappeared into the bush after her infant. The Ranger patrol was extracted shortly afterwards, more than a little shaken by their experience.

During August and September 1969, Bien Hoa Province was awash with torrential rainfall as the south-west monsoon season swept in. In such adverse conditions, the Indiana Rangers were forced to reduce the number of patrols they conducted, but maintained a continuous flow of military intelligence on enemy positions and activities by locating jungle trails and ambushing small units of enemy troops. By the end of October 1969, the size of the reconnaissance zone they patrolled was much reduced and the National Guard membership of the company had dropped below 60 per cent, as the original men from Indiana went back home. On 20 November 1969, the last of the Indiana Rangers departed Vietnam. In their stead, Lieutenant General Julian J. Ewell, commander of the II Field Force Vietnam, formed D Company (Ranger), 75th Infantry, with a cadre of regular army personnel who had been attached to the Indiana Rangers.

With Major Richard W. Drisko in command, the new Ranger company, known as 'Delta Company', was placed under the operational control of the aerial 3rd Squadron, 17th Cavalry, on 1 December 1969. On 8 February 1970, operational control of this unit was transferred to the 199th Infantry Brigade. The unit's surveillance zone was expanded to encompass the former Indiana Ranger area of operations, plus the north-eastern portion of the 'Catcher's Mitt' and western War Zone D in Bien Hoa and Long Khanh provinces.

During their brief period of service, Delta Company made their mark. On 2 December 1969, a team ambush killed a transportation executive officer of the communist Subregion 5 who was carrying the enemy payroll, capturing 30,500 Vietnamese *piastres*. In early January 1970, a nine-man combined ambush group, consisting of Ranger teams 1-4 and 1-5, killed 11 North Vietnamese soldiers from the 274th Regiment of the 5th VC Division. They also sought out that unit's main location, which was subsequently destroyed by shell fire and air attack.

RIVERINE RANGERS

The area around Saigon which included Bien Hoa Province, the 'Plain of Reeds', the Rung Sat Special Zone, and the Mekong Delta, offered a different kind of challenge. The Rangers who patrolled this region evolved from the 9th Infantry Division LRRP Platoon, under Captain James Tedrick. By 8 July 1967, the 9th LRP Detachment had been formalized, and during October of that year it had reached full strength, consisting of a detachment headquarters and two patrol platoons, each composed of a command section and eight six-man teams. Typical of the jungle patrols performed by this unit near Long Thanh, in Bien Hoa Province, was the action involving the team led by Sergeant Hilan Jones during October 1967.

'We had been on patrol for a couple of days', recollected Sergeant Jones. 'I was accompanied by ATL Edward Beckley, Danny Kotsopodis, and two Cambodians. I was impressed with the skills of the Cambodians and took two on patrol whenever they were available. On the second or third day one of the Cambodians developed a severe cough making it impossible to continue our mission, so we called for extraction. We moved to the pick-up zone and were observing a "hooch" about 200 metres from our location while waiting for the choppers. Seeing a couple of people enter it we radioed for

Sergeant Richard Ehrler, E Company, 50th Infantry (LRP), early November 1968, just after returning from a mission to base camp in Dong Tam.
Rick Ehrler

permission to detain them.

'Permission granted, we were moving to take the detainees when we heard voices off to our right about 50 metres away. As we moved to investigate the voices, we discovered they were coming from another hooch. I positioned Beckley, Kotsopodis, and the Cambodians to cover the rear entrance as I moved to the front. As I approached the entrance I could hear the choppers on the way to pick us up. I informed them we would have a detainee waiting when they arrived, I moved to the door of the hooch, and much to my surprise, found eight VC enjoying their lunch of boiled bananas. Their weapons were stacked against one wall, and all but one was sitting together on the slats of the bed. The other one was tending the bananas. When I confronted them to surrender, they all bolted for the rear exit. I yelled to the others that they were coming out, at the same time firing a full magazine into the group. I always liked the WP [White Phospherous] grenade and I tossed one in. The others were shooting the VC who managed to get out the rear.

'The WP marked our position perfectly for the chopper coming to pick us up as well as the gunships who were in support. In a matter of seconds we had eliminated a VC squad, capturing one, before they could fire a single round. Back at Bear Cat, the aero rifle platoon and helicopters of the 3d Squadron, 5th Cavalry were being readied to assault the area. Myself, with Ed and Danny, accompanied them back and led a sweep of the area. As we went through we found eight dead VC, a few pages of documents, 500 pounds of rice, and assorted military gear.' As a result of this action, Sergeant Jones' patrol was credited with knocking out a VC company assembly point of the C240 Local Force Battalion.

On 20 December 1967, E Company (LRP), 50th Infantry, was created to give the 9th Infantry Division specialized ground reconnaissance support. Absorbing the 9th LRP Detachment, the new company, commanded by Captain Clancy Matsuda, was sometimes referred to as 'Reliable Reconnaissance', after the division's preferred nickname in Vietnam—the 'Old Reliables'.

E Company re-structured the six-man patrols to create eight-man teams, and new company volunteers were sent periodically to the MACV Recondo School at Nha Trang. One such volunteer, Sp4 Kenneth R. Lancaster, became E Company's first loss. As part of Recondo student Team 3, led by Special Forces Sergeant Jason Woodworth, he was inserted in hostile territory in Khanh Hoa Province to gain 'live' patrol experience on 3 January 1968. Within hours of insertion, the school operations section received a radio transmission from the patrol requesting extraction as it had become involved in a firefight with the enemy and its position had been compromised. By 0815 hours, a helicopter was hovering over the designated pick-up point, and all team members except Specialists Lancaster and Kozach were able to scramble aboard. After hovering over the LZ for two minutes, the aircraft flew off. Kozach remained at the clearing and waited for another chopper, but Lancaster had grabbed the starboard skid and tried to hang on. The crew did not see him until the aircraft reached a 1,000-foot altitude, near Hon Ong mountain, west of Ninh Hoa. Before the situation could be brought under control, Lancaster disappeared. An extensive search through the jagged jungle mountains failed to locate him. As a result, Kenneth Ray Lancaster remains the only 9th Infantry Division LRP member from the Vietnam War era still missing in action.

During 1968, E Company teams also performed joint operations with Navy SEAL teams to gain training and experience in the Mekong Delta. This involved ambushing armed sampans, initiating 'aquabush' attacks that blocked waterways, and seizing prisoners. An extremely flat region dissected by rivers, numerous tributaries, and canals, the soft soil and silt of the Delta turned into endless mud and flood water during the monsoon season which

lasted from May through October. Torrential rains and year-round water exposed the men to jungle rot, leeches, and all manner of disabling skin disease. The uniform flat and open terrain of the Mekong Delta meant that patrols were exposed when trying to cross wide trackless marshes and fields, while areas of thick underbrush and nipa palms gave the enemy excellent ambush opportunities.

Sergeant Roy Barley recalls the early days of E Company: 'We had perhaps the most difficult of areas to operate in, and did it with success and under very trying circumstances. When I came in, we were primarily in the jungle of III Corps and had a few missions in the Delta. I remember going to the Delta in my first team during late November 1967. We basically ran a few patrols out of the base camp being built there and met with the Seals in My Tho to plan some joint missions in order to see how they operated in that wide open area. I was sent down there permanently after attending the MACV Recondo School in Nha Trang in March 1968. During that time the missions and nature of the operations had changed.'

Hilan Jones recalled: 'Once we moved out of the jungle AO to the Delta our missions changed from 5-7 days to 24-hour operations. We would insert at night from PBRs [Patrol Boat River] and extract the following day depending upon when we were compromised. It was eerie jumping off the bow, in total darkness, not knowing what was ahead. The navy crew had balls of steel. They would come in under heavy fire to pick us out of a hot situation, much like the chopper pilots of D troop, 5th Cavalry'

NIGHT AMBUSH

Rick Ehrler served in the First Platoon, E Company, 50th Infantry (LRP), from April 1968 until the beginning of 1969, when a patrol he led ran into serious trouble. 'January 27, 1969 started out just like many other days for Team 1-7,' he recalled, 'with us preparing for yet another night ambush patrol. We had teams scattered all over the 9th Division

Corporal Mike Kentes, (left) and Sergeant John A. Faracco (right), E Company, 75th Infantry (Airborne). On 24 August 1969, a reaction team including Mike Kentes was inserted in the Plain of Reeds, west of Saigon, after Cobra gunships had shot up a group of enemy personnel spotted heading towards the Cambodian border. During the search, a wounded NVA soldier attempted to unfasten a grenade from his belt, and Kentes shot him with two bursts from his CAR-15. The Ranger later learned that he had killed NVA Lieutenant General Hai Tranh.
Bill Cheek

AO [Area of Operation]. Several months earlier, our teams were kicked off the Mobile Riverine Force (MRF) for smuggling Jack Daniels bourbon on board! Shortly thereafter a VC sapper team swam out to the USS *Westchester County* near Toi San Island with a large quantity of plastic explosives and blew two huge holes in it. We were quickly forgiven and invited to return to the ships.

'We began running ambush patrols along trails and canals within a few klicks of the MRF. In the previous three weeks, we had pulled several effective missions on the south bank area near a major canal intersection called the "cross roads". This area was roughly between My Tho and Ben Tre and consisted of large sections of heavy forest and jungle swamps bordered by kilometres of wide open rice paddies. About half of these missions resulted in contact with a very active local VC force. On this mission, I planned to insert by chopper near a heavy wood line and move the team several hundred metres to a position near one of the canals. Late on that afternoon, I flew over the area in a LOH to pick out some possible sites while on the way to drop off George Calabrese and Chuck Semmit at Ben Tre to be our radio relay. Shortly after returning to the MRF, the Huey arrived and carried six of us off into what turned out to be deep shit!'

At their first insertion point, the team was only

The Ranger's best friend – an AH-1 Cobra gunship of D Troop, 3rd Squadron, 4th Cavalry, which supported both the 1st Division Long Range Patrol Detachment, and later, F Company, 75th Infantry, in all their operations. Note the Centaur insignia painted on its fuselage.
Fred Stuckey

on the ground about 30 seconds before a VC strolled out of the woods 100 metres away. Spotting the Americans, he jumped under cover just as Sergeant Ehrler cut loose with a burst from his M16. It was decided at that point to extract and move a couple of klicks to see if they could get a clean insertion.

'We landed near a small hooch I remembered from a previous mission to be a water buffalo shed,' recollected Ehrler. 'It was almost dark as I scanned the wood line. At that point, I decided it was going to be an interesting night, because there was a Vietnamese man in the woods looking right back at me. When I reported this, I was told we were to keep the mission going anyway.'

The team waited until dark and got under way. After moving cautiously for about an hour, they were still unable to get into the woods due to the heavy movement of people on their way home. Arriving at a cluster of hooches, they occupied an empty one set aside from the others. Ehrler recalled: 'It had thick mud walls, about four feet high, which ran all the way around except for the door opening and a large above-ground bunker of mud and tree trunks. Because of a dry thatch wall on one side, which would have caused too much noise to remove, I had to deploy two men outside on that corner. This should have caused no problem, as they could quickly jump over the wall and knock holes in the thatching if it became necessary. For the next several hours we waited and watched to see what would happen.

'At 2300 hours, I put the team on 50 per cent alert. Richard Thompson, Mark Durham, and Roman Mason took their shot at getting some sleep, while Norman Crabb, Leon Moore and I watched for any activity. Around 2320 hours I thought I saw movement in the woods about 150 meters away. It was a clear night with starlight so bright I could almost read by it. I moved to Moore's position to get the starlight scope. He said there had been no activity on his side of the hooch, away from the wood line. For the next few minutes, Norman Crabb and I observed what appeared to be about 20 people moving around in the woods across from us. I was not overly concerned, because I had claymores set up in that direction.

'Just as I decided to wake the team for possible action and to contact base, I heard voices behind me. Thinking it was Mason and Moore, I grabbed my M16 and started around the hooch to shut them up and get them inside. I had just turned the corner... when I recognized the voices were Vietnamese, and five armed VC stood four feet from me. They were so preoccupied looking down at the sleeping forms of my rear security element, they did not even notice me. I raised my M16 to waste them when I noticed about 20 more VC on the other side of a paddy dyke 10 feet past Mason and Moore's position. I slipped back around the corner and had Crabb cover the closest VC while I moved inside to wake the other guys. I looked over the wall as I whispered into the radio for assistance. We were unable to figure a sure way to wake Mason and Moore and get them in before they would be hit. There must have been at least 20 weapons trained on them at point blank range.'

Contacting his radio relay team, Ehrler was informed the division would not send gunships until the patrol was under fire. Hoping to provide sufficient covering fire to enable Mason and Moore to be rescued, Ehrler next ordered the remainder of his team to 'open up' with everything they had. It failed and the two men were killed where they lay. The mud walls of the hooch held up well as they were now battered by a hail of enemy AK47 rounds, while the thick roof thatching absorbed the blast of several grenades.

'So far, the people I spotted in the wood line had not started firing', remembered Ehrler. 'I figured they wanted us to run from the hooch into their ambush, but I was not about to leave Mason and Moore behind, even if I could. I decided to remove my radio and crawl around the hooch to a point where I could

fire along the right flank of the attacking force, when I spotted more people on my left flank. We were completely surrounded and taking fire from three sides. About that time, an RPG [Rocket Propelled Grenade] came in the door and detonated on the ground three feet in front of me. I think the blast caused me to do a complete back flip while flying about 15 feet across the hooch. For the first few seconds, it felt like someone hit me in the face with a two-by-four, but it quickly numbed into a dull throb. I could not see anything, even though there had been enough light in the hooch before from tracers to see quite well.

'I crawled back across the floor, feeling for my M16 and the radio, when I heard another large blast to my right. Thompson fell to the floor and died almost immediately. Only about five minutes had passed since the first shot, and half my team was KIA, and I was blind. I found my M16 and asked my radio relay team where the Cobras were. I was told they were on the way and "Hotel-Volley 27", the call sign of a 105 battery at fire base "Claw", came up on my frequency and asked if we wanted artillery support. With VC within 10 to 20 feet away and me blind, I said no. I could not pull one of my last two men off the wall long enough to call in 105s on our own heads.

'After about 15 minutes of heavy firing, Crabb

F Company, 75th Infantry (Airborne) had a 'commo' relay station at the top of the the Black Virgin Mountain, or Nui Ba Dinh, just north of Tay Ninh City. According to Fred Stuckey: 'It was generally understood that we owned the top and the bottom of the mountain and the VC owned all the real estate in between. We operated a lot of teams on the mountain. I don't recall anyone completing a mission without contact. It was all one hundred per cent "Indian Country".' *Fred Stuckey*

came to me to say he was out of ammo and Durham was on his last magazine. Since I had been blinded so early in the fight, I had plenty left. I started handing magazines to them and then finally handed my web gear to Crabb after removing a grenade to keep, just in case we were overrun. I noticed that the VC firing was also slacking off and figured they were also running low. I told Crabb and Durham to start shooting semi-automatic at selective targets to keep us going as long as possible. I called once again to ask where the hell our gunships were, and to advise that in a few more minutes they would only need to send graves registration as a reaction force.

'One of the sweetest sounds I can remember hearing was when "Charger 21" told me to mark my position so his gunships could open up. I had Crabb throw my strobe light out the door and said anything more than 20 feet from it was all theirs. The VC that could hauled ass out of there as rockets and mini-guns started tearing up the area. I told Crabb and Durham that we would first drag out our dead teammates when the extraction ship landed, and if there was no effective sniper fire they could go back for our equipment. A chopper crew with balls like King Kong landed in that mess and waited on the ground for us to load. Crabb led me to the bird to keep me from

walking into the tail rotor. The gunships did such a great job of building a wall of lead and fire that we had no problem extracting.

'I spent the next 10 and a half months recovering from wounds and learning how to live as a blind man. Well, it could have been a whole hell of a lot worse.' Sergeant Richard Ehrler was awarded the Silver Star, oak leaf cluster for Purple Heart, and the Vietnamese Gallantry Cross for his courage and bravery on 27 January 1969. His original Purple Heart came from a battle on 21 December 1968, during which he was slightly wounded by another RPG which flew passed his head and detonated on the shield in front of the coxswain's position of a Tango boat. Lieutenant Richard Thompson received a Purple Heart posthumously. It was the second of only two missions he ever pulled.

RANGER KILLS GENERAL

On 1 February 1969, the 'Lurps' of the 9th Infantry Division were re-organized as E Company (Ranger), 75th Infantry. During August of the same year, a 2nd Platoon team operating in Long An Province, west of Saigon, uncovered an enemy Regional Headquarters/Hospital complex in an AO on the Vam Co Tay river. A reaction force subsequently destroyed the complex, but some of its NVA garrison managed to escape and, a few weeks later, were spotted moving towards the Cambodian border. The events that followed produced one of the highest-ranking NVA officers killed in the war.

Thomas P. Dineen, Jr., E Company, recalled: 'On 24 August 1969 my company was working out of Tan An in IV Corps. At about 10.00 hours we were alerted to provide a reaction team to an incident that had developed earlier in the day. It seems that a routine mail chopper en route to Saigon had spotted enemy personnel in the Plain of Reeds and had requested gunships to investigate. The Cobras had fired on a group of enemy and brigade wanted a team on the ground

Hueys from Mackenzie's Raiders, 3rd Squadron, 4th Cavalry, code-named Centaurs 2-4 and 2-6, carry a 13-man heavy combat patrol consisting of Teams 3-8 and 3-9 of the Tropical Rangers, F Company, 75th Infantry on 2 April 1970. Their mission was to destroy an NVA radio team detected in the 'Renegade Woods', north-west of Saigon, in the Hieu Thien District of Tay Ninh Province.
Fred Stuckey

for further surveillance and evaluation. Since no team was available, Sergeant 1st Class Jessie Stevens went through the company area in search of volunteers. Sergeant Chris Valenti, Sergeant Rahamin Bazini, Corporal Mike Kentes, Sergeant Bauza, and myself quickly joined Stevens at the helipad for insertion. We were accompanied by an indigenous mercenary by the name of Kiet.

'Upon reaching the contact site we off-loaded the chopper and began a sweep of the immediate area. There were waist-high reeds and grass through the area, making it difficult to see. We soon came across numerous NVA corpses that obviously had been riddled by the attacking helicopters. Next, we discovered a survivor who was taken prisoner by Valenti. Shortly thereafter we came across another group of bodies with one individual off to one side. As the "corpse" began to move Stevens shouted "*Chieu Hoi*", at which point Kentes noticed that the man was attempting to unfasten a grenade from his belt. Kentes shot him with two bursts from his CAR-15. On searching the body, we discovered a 9 mm Makarov pistol.

'Once we completed the search of the area, we were extracted and returned to Tan An where we turned the prisoner over to Military Intelligence. It was quickly learned that the prisoner had been the personal medic for Lieutenant General Hai Tranh, and that the man Kentes had killed was most likely the general. We were immediately reinserted into the contact area to recover the general's body. When we returned with it, it was confirmed that it was indeed the general!'

Bill Cheek, E Company, recalled: 'I remember waking up to the sound of someone running through the barracks saying "Kentes killed a General! Kentes killed a General!" I groggily remember thinking "Was it one of ours or theirs?" Once the news got out, everyone went over to Tan An airfield to verify the body. I heard that Gen. [Creighton] Abrams and Ambassador Bunker even flew down for confirmation.'

Thomas Dineen, Jr. continued: 'According to our custom, we gave the pistol to the mercenary, Kiet, as sale of captured weapons and equipment was his primary payment for working with us. I later learned that our company commander, Albert C. Zapanta, took the pistol from Kiet.' Major Zapanta recalled of the incident: 'There were 14 bodies and 14 weapons. Three were women armed with M-1 carbines who must have been medics, as they were carrying aid bags. One of the bodies was armed with a beautiful Czech-made Makarov 9-mm pistol—the type carried only by senior officers and officials. Its previous, now dead, owner ended up being Lieutenant General Hai

Tranh, the commander of Military Region 3. I understand it was the only pistol of its type captured in the war. Also recovered were the other weapons and 25 pounds of documents that included a mail sack.'

JUNGLE CLASH

The unit which evolved into F Company (Ranger), 75th Infantry, had its origins in a provisional long range reconnaissance patrol detachment of 41 officers and enlisted personnel formed in 1966 within the 25th Infantry Division and attached to the 3rd Squadron, 4th Cavalry. This unit was also known as 'Mackenzie's Raiders', after Colonel Slidell Mackenzie, who commanded the 4th US Cavalry from 1870 to 1882. Hence, its reconnaissance detachment was nicknamed 'Mackenzie's Lurps'.

The Department of the Army officially authorized the formation of F Company, 50th Infantry Detachment (LRP) on 20 December 1967. This unit was created with the personnel and equipment from the LRRP detachment, and consisted of 118 men including two field platoons composed of seven six-man teams. The new unit adopted the name 'Cobra Lightning Patrollers', after the 25th Infantry Division's nickname 'Tropic Lightning', and its recon teams used the call sign 'Cobra' suffixed by the platoon and team number. The 50th Infantry continued to operate in War Zones C and D, plus the 'Fish Hook', 'Parrot's Beak', and 'Angel's Wing' along the Cambodian border.

Seldom did the combat reconnaissance troops of both sides meet in a firefight during the Vietnam War. When they did, it produced some of the most furious enagagements of the conflict. Late on the afternoon of 29 January 1968, a Cobra Lightning patrol was inserted on the northern edge of Ho Bo Woods, north of Cu Chi, to locate the enemy reported to be moving through that sector and to direct reinforcements into the contact area. Coincidentally, the *élite* Viet Cong 272nd Regiment Reconnaissance Company was serving as the point element for communist columns advancing on Saigon.

At 0425 hours, the two recon forces, composed of some of the most dedicated troops in either army, clashed and the situation escalated rapidly. The Cobra team radioed for the air Rifle platoon of D Troop, 3rd Squadron, 4th Cavalry. The VC called up their own reinforcements. The Rifles were instructed to assist the patrollers in holding on to their position until further help arrived, while VC headquarters ordered their strike force to cover the redirection of their main columns away from the compromised route.

Next page, Ambush at Phu Loi. The Wildcat teams of F Company (LRP), 52nd Infantry, 1st Infantry Division, had twice before mounted short-range ambush patrols from Phu Loi in the direction of 'Dog Leg Village'. On both occasions they had spotted VC/NVA units infiltrating towards Saigon under cover of darkness and successfully called in artillery and air strikes to disrupt them. On the night of 11 May 1968, Teams 1 and 2 once again set up an observation post in a Chinese graveyard surrounded by open paddy fields, and watched the infiltration route through a night vision starlight scope.

Within minutes of taking up position within a pagoda-style monument which offered an excellent vantage point, they spied a battalion-sized enemy infantry unit, followed by a truck mounting a 12.5mm heavy machine gun, coming out of the wood line and heading across open country. For the next few hours, the undetected Wildcats called in artillery and air strikes in a lethal ambush which decimated the foe. At dawn, the LRPs were finally reinforced by seven tanks and ACAVs (tracked armoured cavalry vehicles) from the 1st Squadron, 4th Cavalry, which clanked on to the scene. Scrambling from the graveyard where they had remained undetected, the LRPs formed a skirmish line between the vehicles and swept across the area. Team 1 surrounded a small patch of jungle, and TL Jack Leisure and ATL Roger Anderson went in to search.

In the confusion which followed, they killed four NVA and attempted to capture a wounded enemy officer – but were surprised by a sniper who killed Leisure and wounded Anderson. The rest of the Team, plus a medic from the armoured unit, rushed to their aid, and withdrew under fire carrying the two men. The Cavalry armour next sprayed the area with heavy machine gun rounds and torched it with a flame-thrower. A total of 88 NVA lay dead on the field following this ambush. Though Teams Wildcat 1 and 2 were responsible for detecting the enemy movement, calling in and directing the ambush, and mopping up afterwards, after-action reports credited a Division infantry unit which had not been within 10 kilometres of the location. Many LRP and Ranger operations were 'classified' during the Vietnam War, and this may partially account for the oversight. *Painting by Richard Hook.*

The cavalrymen inserted and managed to link up with the Cobra patrol, and the combined group stared into the late afternoon jungle shadows as the larger VC force stealthily surrounded them. About an hour later, as twilight descended, powerful US airmobile reinforcements composed of the 2nd Battalion, 27th Infantry, 'Wolfhounds', descended on the area and the battle was on. The relief force fought its way doggedly through a wall of tracer-lit enemy fire. The VC recon forces, armed with AK47s and SKS assault rifles, plus the new RPG-2 rocket launchers, offered stiff resistance as they fell back. The Wolfhound battalion finally reached their besieged comrades, who held their ground successfully against all odds. Both sides claimed a victory. The VC advance on Saigon continued via a different route, and the Cobra team and their back-up were successfully extracted. Nonetheless, 64 VC reconnaissance troops lay dead in the jungle after the US troops had departed.

CENTAUR TO THE RESCUE

On 1 February 1969, the personnel plus equipment of the 50th Infantry detachment (LRP) was

This photograph of Tropical Rangers Sp4 Richard Guth, holding his M14 sniper rifle with scope at the ready, was taken by Captain Paul Schierholz, commanding officer, F Company (Ranger), 75th Infantry, aboard Centaur 2-4 just before insertion in the 'Renegade Woods' on 2 April 1970. Note the subdued 25th Infantry Division patch and Ranger scroll on his left shoulder.
Fred Stuckey

reorganised into F Company, 75th Infantry (Airborne). Commanded by Captain Paul C. Schierholz, the three field platoons in this unit were assigned to each of the three brigades of the 25th Infantry Division to collect military intelligence. The three to four teams in each platoon contained eight men, at least one of whom was a qualified sniper. Initially, teams 1-1 to 1-4 supported the 2nd Brigade in Tay Ninh Province. Teams 2-1 to 2-3 supported the 2nd Brigade and teams 3-1 to 3-3 assisted the 3rd Brigade, both of which were in Hau Nghia Province. These teams reached their areas of operation by a variety of means, including foot patrol; helicopter, naval or boat insertion; or armoured personnel carrier. Within highly populated sectors such as that often assigned to F Company, a common mode of entry involved blending with a larger infantry force and then remaining behind after their withdrawal.

On 2 April 1970, the 3rd Brigade commander, Colonel Olin E. Smith ordered Captain Schierholz to send two Ranger teams on a reconnaissance mission into a tactical area called the 'Renegade Woods', located north-west of Saigon in the Hieu Thien District of Tay Ninh Province. Intelligence reports and prisoner interrogation indicated that two main force enemy battalions were moving in to establish a base area from which to conduct offensive operations. An NVA radio transmission, or 'yellow jacket' reading, was also intercepted coming from a specific location there, while enemy structures had been spotted under the trees by a LOH scout helicopter. A long-time enemy stronghold, the 'Renegade Woods' was a large tract of double canopied forest in the middle of open grasslands. The small number of clearings within the dense, vine-choked forest land offered an ideal 'killing zone' during helicopter insertion.

The 13-man combat patrol assembled for the mission consisted of Team 3-8, under Sergeant Colin Hall, and Team 3-9, led by Sergeant Alvin Floyd with First Lieutenant Philip J. Norton in overall command. Armed with normal fire power, plus three M60 machine guns, two M72 Light Anti-tank Weapons (LAWs), and an M14 sniper rifle with scope, the Rangers were under orders to drop into an open area by the transmitter site, destroy it, and get out again. The mission was flown into the region by the Hueys from 'Mackenzie's Raiders', who air-assaulted them into an area close by a large bomb crater, which might afford a degree of cover in an otherwise open landing zone.

The Rangers were inserted at 0835 hours and, approaching the tree line, found signs of recent enemy activity including a large number of footprints and a canvas water bag hanging from a post near a well. Not liking what he saw and wishing to get his men under cover, Lieutenant Norton led his force rapidly along the tree line towards a hedgerow jutting out into the clearing. As Norton and Sergeant Fred Stuckey rounded the end of the hedge, an RPD light machine gun suddenly opened fire at a range of 15 metres. Amazingly, neither men were injured as they dived for cover. Norton landed in a bomb crater approximately 15 feet deep and 30 feet wide, and Stuckey in a smaller shell hole. With incoming fire from all directions, Stuckey and Sp4 Don Purdy, who had worked out from behind the hedgerow, managed to silence the machine gun nest and its occupants with 'frag' grenades.

After calling in air support, Norton decided to vacate the crater and attempt to rejoin his team. Rolling out, he struggled to his feet and started running. Seeing him coming, Sergeant Stuckey left his own cover and, grabbing the officer by the web gear, pulled him behind the hedgerow, where they joined the rest of the team. Meanwhile, the Cobra gunship accompanying the insertion returned and raked the tree line with its mini-gun, and silenced the enemy.

With such heavy enemy presence, Norton felt his mission had been compromised and decided to withdraw his patrol east towards another large clearing in order to conduct an extraction. Radioing Sergeant Floyd and Team 3-9 to provide covering fire to the west, Norton led Team 3-8 out, only to receive fire from another large body of enemy troops hidden in the trees across the other side of the clearing. Deploying in line, the Rangers doggedly fought their way to the opposite tree line, where they discovered and disabled several heavily camouflaged bunkers set back about five metres in the dense undergrowth.

At this point, more VC troops began to appear out of the woods at the far end of the clearing, just as Team 3-9 set out to join their comrades. Fearing Sergeant Floyd had not seen them, Norton attempted to radio him, only to discover that the handset cord on his PRC-25 radio had been severed by gunfire. As Norton looked up, he was horrified to see a B40 rocket sail out of the trees. Hitting Sergeant Floyd head on, it also killed Sergeant Mike Thomas, who was only four days short of the end of his final tour of duty, and seriously wounded Sp4 Donald Tinney.

Norton now shouted for the remainder of Team 3-9 to take cover in the bomb crater, while he ran to Floyd's remains and stripped the radio off his back. Zig-zagging across to the crater, he jumped in and was joined by the rest of Team 3-8. All 10 Rangers were now completely surrounded and running low on ammunition. Furiously, Norton worked to fit the handset of Floyd's otherwise damaged PRC-25 on to his radio, only to find the replacement was clogged with dirt.

Meanwhile, B40 rockets and hand grenades continued to explode along the lip of the crater, wounding a number of those inside. At this stage, Sp4 Don Purdy, whose M16 had been irreparably damaged by enemy fire, grabbed the patrol's two LAWs and fired one at the trees across the clearing. Aiming the second one at another target, he squeezed the firing button but nothing happened. The damp morning air had caused it to jam.

Another RPG machine gun opened up from the infamous hedgerow, and raked the ground around the crater, preventing the Rangers from returning further fire. An NVA soldier emerged from the southern tree line to throw a hand grenade, but was cut down and killed by two hand grenades thrown by Sergeant Stuckey. Pfc Raymond Allmon, carrying one of the three M60s, expended his 700 rounds plus a 50-round belt removed from Sergeant Thomas' body, and was reduced to using his .45 calibre pistol. Pfc Kenneth Langland fired 860 rounds before his M60 malfunctioned, again due to dampness.

Pfc Raymond Allmon and Pfc Steven Perez, Tropical Rangers, on Centaur 2-4 just prior to insertion on 2 April 1970. Little did they know that things were about to go badly wrong as their ambush patrol landed right in the middle of two enemy battalions.
Fred Stuckey

Frustrated by all this, ATL Sergeant Colin Hall sprang to his feet, shouting 'Enough of this shit!' and, jumping out of the crater, charged straight at the VC machine gun nest. Seeing the massive Ranger bearing down on them, the three-man team panicked and ran, only to be cut down by Hall's M16. Dashing back to the crater, he was hit in the side by a sniper bullet. Stopping only to mutter 'Shit!', he threw himself back down on the perimeter and recommenced firing.

Down in the crater, Norton finally managed to get the radio working and requested an immediate extraction, only to be told by Captain Schierholz, circling in the command helicopter, to hold on as available gunships were being withdrawn to refuel and re-arm. Until the fuel level reached critical in their aircraft, the door gunners of the two 'slicks' responsible for the insertion continued to spray M60 fire into the enemy positions as their craft swooped low over the area, helping to draw fire off the Rangers. Listening as Schierholz told the patrol they were to be abandoned, Warrant Officer James 'D. R.' Tonelli, commander of 'Centuar 2-3', one of the Huey 'slicks' still overhead, and a friend of Don

Purdy since Basic Training, advised Lieutenant Norton: 'Suppress your fire – I'm coming in.'

At 0922 hours, pilot Captain Philip Tocco made a low-level approach over the tree tops and landed Centaur 2-3 near the lip of the crater with its tail boom facing the wood line. Furiously, the Rangers began to scramble aboard while Sp5 Charles Lowe, the Crew Chief, maintained M60 fire on the tree line and pilot Tocco fired his .38 revolver through an open window as the VC began to emerge from the undergrowth about 10 metres away. The last man out of the crater, Norton ran for the chopper but stopped momentarily to check Donald Tinney – and found he still had a faint pulse. As he began dragging him towards the 'slick', Purdy and Stuckey turned back to offer help, while door gunner Pfc. Richard Adams, a former 'Tropical Ranger', jumped off the ship to assist in getting Tinney aboard. The four men lifted the limp body into the aircraft, and Purdy slid in after it to cradle Tinney's head on his lap.

With no room left inside the over-crowded cabin, Norton and Stuckey clambered up on the skids and hung on for grim death as the chopper attempted take-off. One of the Huey's- M60 machine guns jammed as it was about to lift off, but several of the Rangers continued to blaze away with their individual weapons as the aircraft took a large number of hits through its cabin floor and rotor blades.

After spending a total of 30 seconds on the ground, the overloaded ship lifted off with maximum torque and severe vertical vibration, and cleared the tree line with 11 Rangers and its crew of four aboard. Centaur 2-3 stopped in a field near Trang Bang to administer initial first aid to Sp4 Tinney, and to redistribute the passengers, before finally landing at the 12th Evacuation Hospital at Cu Chi. The helicopter had received four hits from ground fire during the extraction, and was later examined by experts from Bell Aircraft who expressed amazement that it was still able to fly.

The 25th Infantry Division subsequently airmobiled the 2nd Battalion, 27th Infantry into the battlefield, where it linked up with the 2nd Battalion, 22nd Infantry. The infantrymen discovered that teams 3-8 and 3-9 had inserted in the midst of strongly entrenched elements of the 271st VC/NVA Regiment. The enemy was hurt by this operation, which destroyed the base area of two of their battalions. Fighting continued for another five days, during which 101 enemy were killed, one man was captured and two chose to surrender. US losses amounted to 12 killed and 34 wounded.

Sergeant Alvin Floyd was posthumously awarded the Distinguished Service Cross. Sergeant Michael Thomas and Sp4 Donald Tinney, who died of wounds 10 days later, were posthumously awarded the Silver

Pfc Raymond Allmon advancing forward with his M60 machine gun, with ammunition carrier boxes attached to his waist belt, during the action at 'Renegade Woods'. Sp4 Donald Tinney, at far left, was mortally wounded shortly after this photo was taken.
Fred Stuckey

RANGERS IN ACTION

Star medal. Lieutenant Philip Norton, Sergeants Colin Hall, Fred Stuckey, and Charles Avery also received Silver Stars. The other six Rangers were awarded the Bronze Star with 'V' device.

GOLF RANGERS

G Company (Ranger), 75th Infantry evolved from a LRRP Detachment organised in 1966 by the 196th Infantry Brigade (Separate). This brigade arrived in Vietnam during August of that year, and was assigned to II Corps stationed at Tay Ninh under the command of Brigadier General Richard T. Knowles. It became apparent in the coming months that the 196th needed a far-ranging ground reconnaissance element to gather intelligence on the enemy. On 1 November, General Knowles, ordered the commander of F Troop, 17th Cavalry to form a provisional far-ranging reconnaissance detachment. On 1 December 1966, First Lieutenant John Maxwell volunteered to lead the detachment with Staff Sergeant Earl Toomey as NCO.

Beginning on 2 January 1967, these two leaders interviewed about 200 plus applicants, only 13 of whom were accepted for training and service. These hand-picked men became the cornerstone of the 196th Infantry Brigade LRRP Detachment, which was known as the 'Burning Rope Patrollers' after the 196th Brigade's shoulder patch, consisting of a double-headed burning musket match. This detachment's strength eventually averaged about 40 officers and men.

From February through April 1967, Burning Rope patrols served in Tay Ninh Province, north-west of Saigon. In March, they participated in Operation 'Junction City' as the 196th Brigade joined a push into War Zone C. During this action, a six-man recon team led by Sp4 Robert Webber established a night observation post only five yards from a suspected VC infiltration path. Webber reported that 'a 10-man Viet Cong patrol came upon our rear. We all froze and almost stopped breathing, and the VC went on by us'. Remaining stationary, the patrollers silently watched as other VC troops passed along the trail.

Later that night, the team noticed rustling in nearby bushes and peering through the brush, saw 35 VC soldiers cooking and talking. Pfc William Conner heard further noises to his left and spied three VC walking straight at him. Connor waited anxiously a few seconds to see if they might turn away. When they did not—he opened fire on full automatic, killing the first enemy soldier in the file. Pfc Mark Brennan mowed down the other two men.

As the Patrollers retreated from their hiding place, Pfc Paul Rosselli and Vick D. Valleriano

tossed grenades to cover their withdrawal. Stunned by the sudden assault, the VC did not attempt pursuit, and the recon men were eventually safely extracted. Pfc Connor later remarked of the action: 'We pulled the same tactics Charlie [the Viet Cong] uses: we hit and ran.'

During August 1967, the 196th Infantry Brigade was consolidated into a unit called Task Force Oregon, and by 25 September the latter had been replaced by the 23th Infantry Division (Americal). The Burning Rope Patrollers were finally deactivated on 2 November 1967. Twenty days later, the Americal LRP Detachment (Provisional) was formed at Chu Lai, using assets from several defunct recon groups. Less than a month later, this unit was formalized as E Company (LRP), 51st Infantry. The new company commander was Captain Gary F. Bjork, a graduate of both Airborne and Ranger Schools, and the unit strength was increased from 65 to 118 personnel, with recon teams identified via name brand cigarettes such as Team 'Old Gold', 'Winston', 'Salem', 'Lucky Strike', 'Camel', and 'Marlboro'. The unit's patrol area was expanded to include Quang Ngai, Quang Tin,

Although as yet unpainted, Sergeant Lou Bruchey is otherwise 'saddled up' and ready for a mission as he stands behind the H Company sign at Phouc Vinh in April 1970.

Close-up of reverse of the H Company sign.
Lou Bruchey/Ted Yoshimura

and Quang Nam Provinces. This became the largest operating area for any LRP or Ranger unit in Vietnam.

IRONWOOD TREE

A six-man Americal LRP Detachment reconaissance team led by Staff Sergeant Bob Simpson was inserted into the hills west of Tien Phouc during late November 1967 to establish whether a suspected NVA unit was infiltrating the far reaches of the 196th Infantry Brigade's area of operation. Sergeant Simpson recollected: 'As far as team experience went, we had that, plus – we even had Sgt Don Carter, a Korean War Ranger of some distinction with us. Filling out the team was Bob Wheeler as the radioman; David Ohm was pulling point and "Jolly" Haussler was my ATL.

'We hit the ground on the run, leaning forward under the weight of our heavy canvas rucks, eyes quickly searching for an entrance into the jungle. It was a two-ship insertion, which meant spending nerve-racking time in the area until we could clear the LZ. When all six of us had hit the wood line and moved in a bit, we hit a hasty crouch position, all ears listening for movement. As soon as the sound of the chopper blades dissipated, we could hear a distant but clear gong sounding. They knew we were here, we had to melt into the jungle growth and make tracks fast. GONG, GONG, GONG – the metallic sound reverberated throughout the mountain jungle. My neck hair stood on end; cold sweat soon soaked the cravat around my forehead... .

'The gong finally silenced after about 3-4 minutes, leaving us in relative quiet except for the individual sounds of our heavy breathing, and the soft crunch of our boots on the jungle floor. Stealthily we climbed the mountain seeking a night harbour site to settle into before it got too dark. Blending into the woodwork was our goal, we wanted to hide in the night and remain undetected.

'Our first night was spent uneventfully, no noise, no probing; we made all our radio checks with the radio relay team. Just prior to the break of dawn we saddled up and headed out for a look-see around our assigned block of grid squares. Numerous trails were spotted, fresh signs of recent foot movement and small-sized enemy rest areas were noted along those same trails. We were on to something. Don Carter was chomping at his bit with anticipation; he had packed some extra C-4 in his ruck as he loved the big boom, and he wanted to use it on something, somebody. We continued on, slowly working our way around and down a ridge line; however, we had this feeling we were being followed. Can't explain why, I'm sure others have experienced it at some time or another.'

The team continued with no actual enemy sightings until it was time for extraction. Sergeant Simpson found what looked like a suitable pick-up zone (PZ) on the map, and went with Pfc Ohm to explore it the next morning. The clearing fit the bill, although it was only large enough for one helicopter at a time.

'That situation was not ideal for us, considering there may be unwanted company around,' Simpson recalled. 'Additionally, it had a somewhat large, old gray-looking tree smack in the middle of the clear area. Ohm and I went quickly back to get the rest of the team for our infiltration to the pick-up site; silently we slid into position at the north end. We spread out and scanned the area, all looked and felt secure. I motioned to Carter to join me. When Don had low crawled to my position, I instructed him that I wanted the tree blown; but not until the choppers were inbound. I didn't want to alert the enemy of our location, if they were in the neighbourhood, until the last moment possible.

'"Rattlers inbound." Upon hearing this, Carter, low-crawled slowly, working his way through the elephant grass – we could monitor his progress as the grass waved slightly as he approached the tree. Soon we saw the "wave" coming back toward us; Carter gave us the thumb-up and mouthed, "All Set". All of a sudden there was a tremendous boom, a large cloud of black/gray smoke floated up from the centre of the PZ obscuring the tree. We looked up in horror; the tree shook slightly and then settled down in the full upright, still standing proud and blocking the centre of the clearing. I looked at Carter and yelled, "What the hell happened?" With all the certainty in the world, Carter responded with, "Hell Sarge. It must be an iron wood tree!"

'The lead pilot broke the silence and reported some movement above us on the ridge line. We had to get out of there, as in now. The lead pilot dropped and skilfully manoeuvred his way forward of "Carter's tree", and hung there in a hover while Jolly, Don Carter and the third man jumped aboard. Quickly he pulled pitch; his blades biting the mountain air as he pealed out gaining altitude. And then, all hell broke loose, the ridge line erupted in automatic small arms fire – Wheeler, Ohm and I were now pinned down behind a fallen tree (not the iron wood tree though, for it still stood as a monument in defiance of Carter's skill as a demo man). I grabbed the handset and yelled into the mouthpiece for the other ship to come in and get us. "That's a negative, there's hostile gunfire in the area", was the response heard back. I started to laugh out loud, Ohm looked at me like I was crazy, and at the same time he slid lower behind the fallen tree.

'Now it's rumoured that Jolly held his brand-new "357" to a person's flight helmet, and may have said, 'Tell your buddy to go back and get the rest of my team or else!" It was also rumoured by someone that the pilot said something like, "You wouldn't dare!" This same person recounted that "Jolly" pulled back the hammer and said, "Oh yeah!" Ohm, Wheeler and I can only admit to fact that the second chopper swung in from nowhere and immediately went into a hover with its door guns blazing. We scrambled, all on board, the pilot pulled pitch. The chopper shook and stuttered as we swung around the ridge line in a hasty flight path. Much to his surprise, we caught a fellow in black PJs, with an AK in hand, in the process of trying to jump behind a large rock. Those positioned on the left-hand side of the chopper, the M-60 door gunner and team members, opened up on the poor fellow; he would not live to walk another trail in his Ho Chi Minh sandals, ever again.

'Back in our base camp on the beach, things were hot for a while, "Who pulled the gun?", was the subject of the day. After much discussion, it was chalked up to the combat hype and excitement of the moment – Jolly and I would continue to pull other patrols together. Don Carter never again attempted to down another tree during his tour. Ohm always wondered why I broke out in laughter; I never did have an answer.'

Formed in December 1967, E Company, 51st Infantry was involved in numerous long-range patrol missions that required heavy hunter/killer combat teams in the field, plus sniper missions when required. The unit survived the Tet counter-offensive beginning on 31 January 1968 with minor damage to some of the company's barracks when the Division's ammunition dump exploded from enemy artillery and mortar attack. Between January and September 1968, 15 team members were killed as a result of combat action.

During June, several teams participated as a blocking force during 'Operation Muscatine' in Quang Ngai Province. Also during the same month,

numerous bomb damage assessments were performed, and 50 air strikes were called in on VC-occupied caves and bunkers. Team Winston managed to photograph a T55 Russian tank in the hedgerow north-east of Duc Pho close to the Laotian border. Another team, under the leadership of Sergeant Ben Dunham, captured a Chinese national with the rank of colonel.

On 1 February 1969, E Company, (LRP) was reorganized as G Company, 75th Infantry (Airborne). Commanded by Captain Anthony Avgoulis, the unit was authorized 118 soldiers, organised into a company headquarters of 18, and two 50-man field platoons, each with eight six-man patrols and a two-man headquarters component. Team names were changed to reflect states of the Union, such as 'Hawaii', 'Ohio', and 'Texas'. The unit was assigned to the 16th Aviation Group, which provided helicopter transport, plus aerial and ground assistance.

G Company was accredited with the location of more than 8,000 enemy soldiers, numerous enemy base camps, infiltration and supply routes, plus weapon caches and training sites. It conducted no

Door gunner in a chopper belonging to the 1/9th Assault Helicopter Squadron prepares to extract an H Company team in Long Khanh Province during December 1970.
Ted Yoshimura

less than 662 combat operations, resulting in 322 confirmed enemy kills, 106 enemy wounded in action, and 53 prisoners of war. The unit participated in the defence of 'Firebase Fat City', 'LZ Baldy', and Chu Lai base, and indirectly came to the support of every battalion-sized combat group in the Americal Infantry Division.

On 13 May 69, 'LZ Baldy' was attacked by an NVA sapper force, and the 196th Infantry Brigade was pushed off the Landing Zone. During the initial fighting, most of the Rangers of 'Texas' and 'Michigan' teams were wounded but fought back and drove the enemy off, killing 40 NVA troops. During interrogation, a captured NVA officer stated he had been trained in China and ordered to destroy the Rangers who, he reported, had caused major disruption to NVA/VC routes of movement from North Vietnam into Laos/South Vietnam. His force had failed to destroy the 'men with the bounties on their heads.'

SAVING HIS TEAM

On 14 November 1969, Staff Sergeant Robert Pruden led Team 'Oregon' on a trail surveillance mission west of Duc Pho, deep inside enemy-occupied territory in Quang Ngai Province, during which they ambushed 10 VC dressed in black peasant clothing and civilian attire. Returning four days later to conduct a prisoner snatch, the team was inserted on a hill and disappeared down into the rice fields, after which it established two three-man positions alongside the enemy route. As they laid down their claymores, 12 VC appeared and the team froze until they had passed by. Assuming all was clear, a team member crawled forward to continue placing his claymore, when he was spotted at a distance by enemy soldiers who immediately opened fire and pinned him down.

Realizing that the ambush position had been compromised, Sergeant Pruden directed his team to open fire on the enemy force. The team immediately came under heavy fire from a second enemy element. With full knowledge of the extreme danger involved, Pruden left his concealed position and, firing as he ran, advanced toward the enemy to draw the hostile fire. The VC were initially startled, but quickly turned their attention on the charging Ranger. Pruden was hit several times and knocked

Rangers of H Company, 75th Infantry (Airborne) accompanied by a combat photographer on patrol near Phuoc Vinh in Phuoc Long Province in February/March 1971. Team Leader Ron Williams is walking 'point', Lieutenant Denker follows behind as 'slack', with Ted Yoshimura third in line.

During an otherwise uneventful mission, the men form a 'security wheel' during a rest stop. Note the Ranger scroll and 1st Cavalry Division patch on the shoulder of the man on the left.
Ted Yoshimura

to the ground, but regained his footing and struggled on until wounded again. Falling at the edge of the trail, he reloaded his weapon and staggered once more to his feet, firing as he went on. With four of their own men killed by Pruden's sub-machine gun fire, the VC fled.

As they disappeared into the jungle, they turned and hit the Ranger one more time. Pruden finally fell with five bullet wounds in the chest and abdomen. Running to his aid, the Rangers established a perimeter around their stricken Team Leader who, despite his weakening condition, continued to give directions to his men and managed to call in extraction choppers, after which he lost consciousness and died. Several minutes later, the extraction aircraft arrived overhead, and Team 'Oregon' was lifted out. Staff Sergeant Robert J. Pruden was posthumously awarded the Medal of Honour for giving his life to protect his team members during the mission at Duc Pho.

CAVALRY RANGERS

The forerunner of H Company (Ranger), 75th Infantry was the provisional long range reconnaissance patrol detachment formed within the 1st Cavalry Division between December 1966 and February 1967. Established despite Major General John Norton's belief that the Cavalry already had a reconnaissance capability, this unit was commanded by Captain James D. James, who was ably assisted by 1st Sergeant Ronald Christopher. Sergeant Christopher, a Reconnaissance Intelligence Specialist and Ranger Staff Sergeant with combat experience in a recon unit, became Team Leader, Team One, 1st Cavalry Division LRRPDs.

'Our missions were seven days in duration with one day off, then we had to go back out,' he recalled. 'My first overflight was done in a B Troop, 9th Cav gunship. The second overflight was conducted from the right seat of a Mohawk and my third took place from the back seat of a Bird Dog. We also conducted our insertions with one chopper. It was the only one we had. The only training my team received was what I gave them, compass, map reading, patrolling techniques... We carried a basic load of ammunition. We had no grenades, claymore mines etc. We inserted in at dark 30 and we were extracted on the morning of the eighth day. Our mission was recon intell, period. We had no support, no reaction force back-up, no artillery, gunships, nothing. James informed me just prior to our loading on the chopper for the first mission, "This is a 'do or die' mission. If you don't stay in the An Lao, there will be no LRRP."'

On the success of these first missions, other LRRP detachments were organised throughout the 1st Cavalry Division. Team One was attached to the

1st Brigade, which continued to operate in the An Lao Valley, while a second team worked the Kim Son Valley with the 2nd Brigade. These units provided invaluable patrol support during 'Operation Pershing', an 11-month search-and-destroy campaign which covered most of Binh Dinh Province.

Sergeant Christopher recalled: 'On one mission we had covered the entire area of operation and were at the PZ the evening prior to pick up. On my map, prior to insertion, I had marked an X in a valley that I wanted to check, if we had the time, and I was going to check it the last day because it was located down the mountain from the pick-up zone. We headed out and I took the lead because my instincts told me that the valley was heavy with someone, be they the enemy or not, but in the jungle, who the hell was the enemy?

'I led the team down this trail, time was vital because we had to get back up so we could meet the pick-up chopper. I smelled smoke so I had the team get off the trail and hide in the underbrush. Poppa, son and wife with two small kids came walking down the trail, poppa and son smoking a pipe. He was a hamlet chief, a long white scarf hung down from his waist. We followed him down the trail. There was a curve in the trail which I eased around, my back up against the high brush lining the trail, and walked right smack into a hamlet. Standing there were two children, a boy and a young girl. What was I to do now? I walked right into the hamlet, begged for water while motioning for my team to back away and head up the trail, quickly. I followed, covering. We got pretty far up the trail when this girl lets out with an ear-piercing scream, and up out of the valley below came the horde!

'It was a mad rush to get to the PZ and the thoughts as to who would get there first – the enemy or the chopper. Somehow they both seemed to arrive at the same time but I wouldn't let the chopper set down due to the high grass. I jumped up and grabbed a skid and then pulled my men up and over me and pushed them into the chopper. The door gunner on the other side opened fire and was killing the enemy as they came out of the jungle and into the opening. This was a later mission and my scout carried an M79. He let loose with a round and, believe it or not, it went right into an enemy's mouth, blowing his head off. I was shooting at the enemy while hanging from a skid and screaming up at Fletcher to tell the pilot to get us the hell out of there!'

In April 1967, Major General John J. Tolson III assumed command of the 1st Cavalry Division, and expanded the provisional LRRP unit into the 1st Division Long Range Patrol Detachment (LRPD), which now had a strength of 118 US Army soldiers,

18 Montagnard tribal warriors, and 18 South Vietnamese scouts. During the summer of 1967, from three to nine teams served interchangeably within the two brigade sectors, achieving numerous sightings and initiating several contacts with small VC and NVA elements.

The most significant intelligence windfall of 'Operation Pershing' was achieved by the Cavalry LRPs on 5 December 1967. A team inserted to search the jagged mountains of the Suoi Ca Valley the previous day, ambushed three VC wearing green uniforms. Killing one and capturing the other two, the prisoners were flown to the division interrogation centre, where it was revealed that the patrol had intercepted an important delegation from the communist Binh Dinh provincial headquarters. One of the prisoners was identified as a senior VC intelligence captain just returned from a two-year course of indoctrination in the Soviet Union. The dead VC was found to have been a battalion executive officer. The 1st Cavalry Division gained valuable information on enemy organisations, plus plans and strategies, from their captive. During the last few months of 1967, the LRRP detachments carried out a further 105 patrols and notched up 350 enemy sightings from their bases at Phan Thiet, 'Landing Zone English', and 'Landing Zone Uplift'.

On 20 December 1967, the 1st Cavalry Division LRRP detachments were absorbed into E Company (LRP), 52nd Infantry, and were activated at Camp Radcliffe outside Ahn Khe, under the command of Captain George A. Paccerelli. The new unit was scattered over a wide area when the surprise VC Tet-68 offensive struck. Only a few teams could be spared to disrupt North Vietnamese supply lines leading to the Quang Tri and Hue battlefields. Nine were retained to protect Binh Dinh Province and assist 2nd Brigade monitor VC activity in the Crescent, Nui Mieu, and the Cay Giep mountains. The remaining teams were held on guard duty outside the main perimeter of 'Camp Radcliffe' itself.

During the fall of 1968, the 1st Cavalry Division, and its 'Lurps', were relocated south to the III Corps Tactical Zone, in order to help screen the approaches to Saigon. There they adjusted to a new operational area consisting of jungle plains, rice fields, and marshy swampland, much of which was highly populated.

Clashes with the enemy increased during December 1968. On the 13th of that month, Team 3-9, commanded by Staff Sergeant Ronald J. Bitticks, ran into a large NVA force four miles north-west of Phuoc Vinh. While examining a pathway, point man Sergeant Edward Malone spied two enemy soldiers approaching. Deciding on a prisoner snatch, Bitticks signalled his intentions to the rest of the team and stepped on to the trail barking, '*Chieu Hoi!*' He recalled: 'It was evident by the surprised expression upon their faces that they didn't believe what they saw. For a few seconds they just stared; then they went for their weapons. I opened up with my M16, killing one while the other managed to escape into the bamboo thicket.'

Advancing after him as quietly as possible through the dense foliage, Team 3-9 found themselves back on the same trail, where they saw a much larger enemy force approaching. Realizing his team's position was untenable, Sergeant Bitticks radioed out for air support. Ten minutes later the Cobras arrived overhead and the patrollers, who were by now surrounded, popped several smoke grenades to mark their position, while the aircraft repeatedly strafed the enemy. 'This went on for over two hours', recollected Sergeant Bitticks. 'If if hadn't been for the gunships we never would have got out alive. At one point a machine gun opened up on us from only 25 feet away. It cut a path between us, raking our position first horizontally and then vertically, slitting the bamboo all around us.'

Advancing closely behind three gunship runs which were carefully co-ordinated by Bitticks, the team broke out of its encirclement and struggled

Opposite, **two painted warriors of H Company (Ranger), 75th Infantry (Airborne). 'Tex' Williams (left) holds a calibre .45 M3A1 submachine gun, while 'Wild' Jim Massengill (right) is armed with a Soviet 7.62 mm AK assault rifle. Note that both men have ties below their knees to prevent bugs, reptiles and blood-sucking leeches from crawling up their trouser legs.**
Glen McCrary

Right, **the face of the enemy. On 22 November 1970, an H Company Heavy Team set up an ambush along a stream when they heard the sounds of voices and a transistor radio coming from the opposite bank. Crawling up on the enemy position, the Rangers engaged them, resulting in two enemy dead, and the following captured items: five AK-47s, three** K-54 pistols, one P-38 pistol, uniforms, personal gear, and a camera containing a film. When the film was developed, it contained a photograph of this VC soldier holding an AK assault rifle and a mixture of NVA and US web gear. Note the tunnel flash light attached to his waist belt.
Glen McCrary

to a small pick-up zone in the jungle. Under the continued covering fire of the gunships, they furiously hacked down trees with their machetes to make a clearing large enough for extraction. The bravery of the team members and supporting helicopter crews combined to keep a much larger enemy force at bay, and Team 3-9 was lifted out safely that evening.

On 1 February 1969, E Company (LRP), 52nd Infantry, was deactivated and its personnel were absorbed into H Company, (Ranger), 75th Infantry. This unit continued to be assigned to the 1st Cavalry Division, and remained at Phuoc Vinh in Binh Duong Province, north of Saigon, under the operational control of the 1st Squadron, 9th Cavalry.

During the build-up to the Tet offensive of 1969, H Company provided invaluable reconnaissance data on enemy units moving through the jungles and along canals and waterways. With an increased enemy willingness to stand and fight, they also called in numerous team-directed air strikes and artillery bombardments, and provided reaction forces for those patrols involved in fire fights.

SLASHING TALON

During the invasion of Cambodia between April and June 1970, H Company conducted 50

Lou Bruchey, Team Leader of H Company Team 'Slashing Talon 7-4' firing his M-16 in the Pick-up Zone while waiting for extraction. Known as 'recon by fire', it was done to make sure the enemy was not hiding in the bush waiting to jump the Rangers as they climbed on board the helicopter.
Lou Bruchey

reconnaissance missions and provided the 1st Cavalry Division with numerous intelligence reports. Lou Bruchey, who volunteered for Ranger service shortly after his arrival in Vietnam during January 1970, became Leader of Team 'Slashing Talon 7-4', and recalled: 'One of my most hair-raising incidents occurred during the US invasion of Cambodia in May of 1970. I was on one of the first teams to lead the 1st Air Cavalry Division into Cambodia. On the second day of our first mission, we were set up in an overnight position just inside a tree line, monitoring a trail located several metres out into a large open area which ran parallel to the tree line. Just as it began to get dark, several hundred metres up the tree line a column of NVA soldiers began streaming out of the woods and moving down the trail towards our position.

'They marched by us in groups of 20 to 50 over a span of about an hour. There were so many that we couldn't accurately count them all, but later we estimated the number to be several hundred. They were heavily laden with packs, equipment, and weapons, and jabbered freely as they passed our position less than 10 metres away. Incredibly, as one group passed us, US artillery opened up in the distance. Fearing the NVA would rush into the tree line for protection, we quietly radioed the firebase to cease fire. When we felt the last of the NVA had passed, we radioed our artillery with the co-ordinates of the area where the enemy was heading. That was one of the most amazing nights of my life. I felt like I was actually in a Hollywood war movie. To see and hear that many enemy soldiers so close to our position was unbelievable. Our camouflage and sound discipline literally saved our lives.'

On a mission in Phuoc Long Province, south of Song Be, during February 1971, Japanese-American Sergeant Ted Yoshimura also had a very close encounter with the enemy. Serving as the 'tail-gunner' as Team '3-2' took up a trail observation point, he remembered: 'I continued to watch the trail as everyone settled down. I finally sat down with my pack also to the outside of our perimeter. Our Team Leader [Ron Williams] instructed us to chow down at this time. I was waiting for the others to get situated and remove their Lurp rations from their packs. My arms were still in my rucksack straps and it was difficult to turn in the direction of the trail. I was still partially exposed and was trying to figure out my predicament for more concealment. I didn't see or hear any movement on the trail. I had just turned my head to see how the team was doing and I suddenly caught movement in my peripheral vision.

'I slowly turned to see a single NVA soldier carrying an AK-47 with the 30-round clip hanging below the receiver. As he stepped off the trail in my direction, I wasn't sure what do. Now, everything seemed to be going in slow motion. I almost couldn't believe what I was seeing. I remember thinking after being extracted that he must have been hiding in the thick brush as we crossed the trail. The enemy soldier appeared to be about 5' 8" tall. Taller than what I was accustomed to and looking well groomed – even his uniform seemed to be clean. He was approaching from my left rear. I was certain that he saw me because we made eye contact. I was the only person on the team exposed

from our position and I couldn't just grab my AK-47, take my weapon off safety, turn in his direction and shoot him. It was just too much of a threatening movement. Besides, he already had the drop on me, and on the team.

'With my right leg, I began lightly tapping Ron's boot. Fortunately, his foot was convenient and he was sitting directly across from me. He would be able to get a straight shot on the gook. It felt like I had kicked him a couple of dozen times with no response. In unison with my foot I was whispering, "Gook! Gook! Gook!" I thought I was going to take a shot to the back!'

'The NVA soldier must have been about 10 feet behind me by this time. When I finally got Ron's attention, he immediately realized what I was trying to tell him.... He slowly reached for his M-16 and in a single motion, rotated the selector switch to full auto as he dove between me and the next guy. I remember feeling the blast of the automatic fire on my body as the rounds left the muzzle. At the same moment, I rolled over, threw my selector switch to full auto and hosed down the area where I thought the gook would be plus the surrounding area. I replaced my empty magazine and continued to spray the surrounding area in my fire zone; and everyone else's fire zone too. I was looking for the

When available, LRPs and Rangers used AN/PVS-2B Starlight Scopes to give them night time vision.
Author/Alex Allen and Neil Holdom

Next page, Time for a mission. A four-man K Company Ranger team heading for a helipad near 'Firebase Blackhawk'. Second from left, carrying a PRC-25 radio, is team leader Louis Nieves-Munoz, of Panama. The man in the Boonie hat at far left is Jacob Ruiz of Chicago. *Larry Flanagan*

body and again replacing my empty magazine but I couldn't locate one. I thought I spotted some movement in the brush along the trail and fired about a half magazine in that direction. Finally, a PINK Team [Light Observation Helicopter and Cobra Gunship] came on station for our air support and extraction… .

'When we were all finally in the chopper, the LOH pilot mentioned that he spotted a couple of bodies right off the trail. We headed back to our base camp in Phuoc Vinh. It was customary for a team to get a steak dinner whenever they got a kill. I can't remember eating steak that night and I probably didn't care. I probably went to the company bar for a drink.'

On 18 October 1970, Sergeant Bruchey's team was inserted in a remote jungle area in III Corps Tactical Zone, near Song Be (2nd Brigade), called the Dragon's Head. 'After our team made initial contact with an unknown size enemy force, I crawled forward and assaulted the enemy position with M-16 fire and hand grenades', he recollected. 'We found four dead enemy soldiers. Quickly, we stripped the bodies of weapons, documents, and souvenirs; then we left our calling card – the wooden nickel.

'However, we realized this was the lead element of a larger enemy force, and we called for a platoon quick-reaction force known as the "Blues".

'After the Blues arrived at a nearby landing zone, they were ambushed as they approached our position, pinned down, and suffered several casualties. Unable to move, the Blues radioed our team to move to their position and link up. When we linked up with the Blues, we helped evacuate the wounded who were lifted through a small opening in the canopy by a jungle penetrator to a hovering medivac helicopter. After aerial fire support from Cobra gunships, we were able to disengage from the enemy and our LRRP team led the Blues to an LZ where we were all extracted just before nightfall.

'Throughout my tour, we lost men because of death, wounds, injuries, transfers, and disease [usually malaria]. However, from my experience with H Company, I realized it was just as easy to get killed or injured in non-combat as it was to get killed or wounded in combat. During my first month with the unit, we had one Ranger (a member of my class) fall to his death from a jungle penetrator during a night extraction. Another Ranger was cut in half when he was hit by a rotor blade from a chopper during a botched insertion. We even had a Ranger severely injured during a mission when a tree, weakened by agent orange, toppled onto him during a thunderstorm.

'I was nearly killed twice just doing things Rangers do in the field. On the first occasion, my D-ring came loose when I was hanging on to a McGuire Rig 120 feet beneath a chopper at an altitude of approximately 1500 feet, travelling at 100 knots. With a pack, weapon, and web gear, I hung on to the rope for about 20 minutes until the chopper finally touched us down.

'The second instance occurred during a night extraction by McGuire Rig, when the chopper pilot on his approach to a firebase flew me into a 10-foot stack of steel plates used for temporary landing strips. The impact shattered my M-16, tore me from the McGuire Rig, sliced open my head, bruised my ribs, and put me in the infirmary and on light duty for several weeks.

'Crazy things happened in Nam. Although nearly every mission was in active enemy territory, some guys went on patrol after patrol and never made contact. Others seemed to run into gooks as soon as they got off the chopper. We had one kid who got shot on his first patrol. He was in the unit such a short time I never knew his name. His team was inserted into an area of operation, walked off the LZ and set up to make a commo check. Several metres away, a gook pops up and fires a burst into the Rangers, hitting the kid in the chest. The insertion chopper hasn't even left the area yet, so it comes back down and the whole team, including the kid, runs back out to the LZ and gets extracted. The kid gets medivaced to a hospital and sent home with a Purple Heart; his war is over after only minutes in the field.'

WILDCATS SAVE PHU LOI

During April 1966, Major General William E. DePuy, commander of the 1st Infantry Division ('The Big Red One'), formed a provisional division Long Range Reconnaissance Patrol contingent to operate north and west of Saigon. Attached to D Troop, 1st Squadron, 4th Cavalry, the unit became known as the 'Wildcat Lurps', after their call sign 'Wildcats'. On 28 September 1967, this group was formalized as the Long Range Patrol Detachment, 1st Infantry Division, with an authorised reconnaissance personnel of 118, which consisted of headquarters and operational sections, and two patrol platoons, each composed of eight patrols of six men. Commanded by Captain Jack Price, the Wildcat Lurps officially became F Company (LRP), 52nd Infantry on 20 December 1967.

On 31 January 1968, Team Wildcat 2 led by Sergeant Ronnie Luse was manning a forward night observation post in a Chinese graveyard outside Phu Loi, headquarters for the 1st Infantry Division's artillery, armoured cavalry, and other key units, when they detected an estimated VC/NVA regiment emerge from the woods and start across the rice paddies towards the village of An My. Luse hurriedly radioed the division tactical operations centre: 'I see a large number of Viet Cong on line moving towards us–several hundred of them!' Calling in an artillery ambush, the Lurps remained in position as a 'Firefly' team, consisting of a Huey helicopter specially equipped with a powerful Xenon searchlight, flooded the fields with artificial light. As they hugged the trembling ground, the patrollers adjusted 105mm howitzer and aerial fire which virtually decimated the enemy, and drove the remnants into An My. Team 'Wildcat 2' had detected and foiled the main Viet Cong Tet-68 offensive against the 1st Infantry Division. Sergeant Luse was awarded a Silver Star for the initiative he displayed that night.

After the Tet Offensive battles of 1968, the F Company 'Lurps' became involved in a continuing campaign to weaken VC infiltration corridors running past Phu Loi towards Saigon. After dark on 11 May, Teams Wildcat 1 and 2 occupied the same miniature pagoda-style monument in the graveyard used by Team 2 on 31 January. Offering an excellent field of vision about five feet above the surrounding paddies, they settled down with a night scope to see if lightning could strike twice in the same place. It did! Within minutes they once again spied a battalion-sized enemy unit, followed by a truck mounting a 12.5mm heavy machine gun, coming out of the wood line and crossing via the same route used in January. For the next few hours, the LRPs remained undetected as they called in artillery strikes in a lethal ambush which decimated the foe. Just before dawn, enemy rocket and mortar fire was heard in the direction of Phu Loi, and shortly afterwards a US spotter plane reported another large NVA force heading towards the area. During a hiatus in shell fire, most of the NVA that could still move began to vacate the rice paddies. The LRPs requested permission to conduct a sweep across the battlefield before the survivors could escape, but were told to 'sit tight until the Cav arrived'.

An hour after sunrise, the LRPs were finally reinforced by three tanks and four ACAVs (tracked armoured cavalry vehicles) from the 1st Squadron, 4th Cavalry. Forming a skirmish line between the armour, they advanced towards the target area. Shots rang out as survivors attempted to retaliate. Several prisoners were taken and moved at gun-point over to helicopters waiting to take them in for interrogation. But the lapse in artillery fire had obviously allowed the NVA to move many of the dead, wounded, and weapons from the open rice paddies. The LRPs and their small armoured escort

would have to continue their sweep if contact was to be regained with the badly hurt enemy force.

Half an hour later, they spotted enemy stragglers running in several different directions and decided to split their Teams for pursuit. Sergeant Luse and most of Team 2 jumped up on the back of a tank and sped north after a group fleeing towards An My. Team 1, led by Sergeant Jack Leisure, rode eastward in similar fashion after another group running toward Dog Leg village. ATL Roger Anderson of Team 1 recalled: 'About 10 minutes later the lead tank stopped and the crew said they thought they saw movement in a small patch of jungle. Leisure and I jumped off the tank, and went looking. Suddenly we saw four guys standing like statues looking at the tank. They didn't see or hear us. So we let loose and dropped the four of them, two were wounded but dying fast. In the meantime Elsner went in through the back door of a hooch and found a field aid station. There was one old wounded guy separate from the rest who looked like an NVA officer. Leisure and I were searching the bodies of the four guys when Elsner came out and told us what he found. Leisure said: "C'mon, Andy, let's go get him". I told the captain from the Cav to give us a medic and off we went. We found the guy all right. The next thing I knew, we were under fire and he came flying back at me screaming: "Oh my God, Andy!"

'I got the safety off my M14, but before I could get a shot in, I was spinning like a top! I landed on my right side and all I could see was a really light shade of green. As I went down, I remember screaming, "Oh, my God, I'm dying!" Suddenly my left leg shot straight up in the air, and I reached up and grabbed it. I opened my eyes and realized I was alive. My rifle was laying to my left. I went to grab it, but my hand was mangled. My trigger finger looked like somebody made a cross section of a finger and my thumb was hanging by a little piece of skin. While the guy decided to reload, I grabbed it left-handed, and fired where I saw the bushes flicker. I put four duplex rounds through his chest.'

Anderson attempted to load a fresh magazine into his weapon, but found that his spare magazines had been shot up, probably saving his life as they absorbed some of the rounds which hit him in the back. Unable to move due to his wounds, he could only stare at the wounded NVA officer they had originally gone after. 'The guy we were going to take prisoner and I stared at each other for a short time and we both felt bad for each other,' he recollected. 'He had a 9 mm pistol and could have done me, but chose not to.' The rest of the Team hurried over to offer cover, while the Cav medic tried vainly to resuscitate Leisure. After the LRPs and medic had withdrawn, carrying the two men, the Cav armour sprayed the area with heavy machine gun rounds and torched it with a flame-thrower to complete their sweep. A total of 88 NVA lay dead on the field following the action.

COBRA GUNSHIP EXTRACTION

On 18 June 1968, four men of Team Wildcat 2 led by Pfc Robert P. Elsner were conducting a two-day reconnaissance mission near Ap Go Cong, a village long suspected of being a VC sanctuary in the 'Catcher's Mitt' area north-east of Saigon. During the darkness of the first evening, the team was setting up to observe a trail running across a rice paddy towards the village, when Elsner got the feeling they were being watched. Using a Starlight scope to peer through the gloom, he detected enemy troops, with several tripod-mounted machine guns, deploying around them on opposite sides of the clearing. Advising his team they had "gooks all around them", they hastily formed up in a 'wheel' – feet to the centre, with each man covering his assigned sectors of fire. Five claymore mines were quickly put out in a circle around them. Rather than give their position away by opening fire, Elsner ordered "Grenades only, no shooting". Each man crawled out as far as possible, and lobbed a fragmentation grenade in the direction of the enemy – but for some reason the VC did not respond.

Elsner next called in artillery and air support. Requesting a marker round at the first concentration, he advised the artillery battery's Fire Direction Centre that the range would need to be "danger close" to the team's own position to be of any value. A first attempt failed to produce any incoming rounds, and on the second attempt the team spotted a flash so far away that they barely heard its sound. Something was wrong with the co-ordinates. Elsner was just about to try a third time when a voice suddenly broke in over his radio: 'Wildcat 2, this is Dark-Horse 32'. Lieutenant Larry Taylor, piloting a Cobra gunship, was trying to establish contact with the team. That night Taylor was the Flight Leader of a two-ship flight of Cobras from D Troop (Air), 1st Squadron, 4th Cavalry, which had scrambled out of Phu Loi in response to the team's predicament. Elsner felt momentary relief. The pilots of the 'Quarter-Cav', as the unit was known throughout the 1st Division, had never let the LRPs down, and they were now clearly on the way to help the team.

Elsner immediately cancelled the artillery, deferring to Taylor for any further calls for artillery support. He then switched to the gunship frequency and gave the pilot a sit-rep. He advised Taylor that he would get him started in the right direction upon sighting his lights. When the gunships were close, the team would fire 'star-clusters', or hand-fired flares, over the known and suspected enemy positions. With this established, Taylor re-confirmed the co-ordinates of the location on his map and advised the artillery that he would require artillery flares on his command, in order that the enemy forces could be revealed and destroyed.

Advised by Taylor that he was almost on station, the LRPs launched their star-clusters and all hell broke loose as everyone began firing at once. The two Cobras swooped down on either side of the team's position and hit the tree lines on each flank with 2.75-inch rockets. Taylor then flew back round and sprayed with mini-gun fire a gully the VC were seen using to approach the LRPs. For the next half an hour or so, the gunships kept up their forays, but the enemy, who began to receive reinforcements, also maintained their fire despite taking awful casualties. Meanwhile, the LRP team hugged the ground as they lay behind the sun-hardened earthen rice paddy berms which thankfully absorbed most of the enemy incoming fire.

After having fired a total of 152 rockets and nearly 16,000 rounds from their mini-guns, the Cobras were almost out of ammunition, while enemy fire remained incessant. Seeing the gunships execute several dry runs, the VC realised the situation and increased their fire rate on the trapped LRPs. Convinced that the team would soon be overrun, Taylor advised Elsner to prepare for escape and evasion across the gully and out into the open country. Timed to coincide with a final gunship run using the remaining mini-gun rounds, the LRPs would blow all their claymore mines and then use fire-and-manoeuvre tactics to make their way further out into the large rice paddy.

Though the team did not yet know it, Taylor had decided to extract his beleaguered comrades on his Cobra, which had no internal cargo hold. When the pilot radioed his plan to headquarters, he was ordered by successively higher-level ground commanders not, under any circumstances, to expose his valuable ship and crew in such an unorthodox manoeuvre. He was told that, since the 'Lurps' were now committed to escape and evade across the rice paddies towards a river, they would just have to continue with that strategy until they were extracted in the standard manner by a Huey helicopter. Immediately and in no uncertain terms, Taylor responded that he was "exercising his prerogative as the senior on-scene commander and was proceeding with the Cobra extraction, regardless of the consequences."

The pilot stopped all artillery illumination rounds,

except those he had ordered on the nearby village, and upon his command the team detonated their claymores and moved out, each man firing up his designated area of responsibility and covering each other. They immediately came under increased fire from the tree line to their south and the village behind them, but kept running and firing. Once they had crossed the gully, Sergeant William P. Cohn Jr. dropped off with his M-79 to lay down covering fire for the rest of the team. Sergeant David Hill, on rear security, fired a final magazine at the VC in the village and passed through Cohn's position as the rest of the team ran further into the rice paddy.

The team had gone nearly 100 metres when they suddenly felt a powerful blast of warm air and noise coming from directly overhead. It was Taylor's gunship hovering over them without any running lights. Suddenly realising that Cohn had still not caught up with the team, Hill turned and screamed for him to catch up. As Cohn leaped to his feet and began running, he failed to see two VC closing down on him. Both Elsner and Hill immediately opened fire on the enemy and took them out. At that point, the Cobra was still hovering 50 feet up in the night sky above the team. Just as Cohn arrived, Taylor dropped his ship to the ground 10 metres from the team's position and frantically motioned for the LRPs to climb aboard.

Looking at the pilot and then each other, they thought the pilot must be insane, but then figured it out and quickly ran to the Cobra. Given the grim alternatives, Taylor knew the LRPs would devise a way of securing themselves to his aircraft. Cohn and Hill continued around to the other side of the Cobra, each climbing on to, and straddling, one of the rocket pods, while gripping the leading edge of the ordnance pylon. On the other side, Elsner quickly snapped the extended antenna off Sp4 Gerald Paddy's radio, and each fired off a final magazine at the enemy weapons flashing in the tree lines behind them. As the aircraft began to lift slowly off its landing skids, the two LRPs still on the ground secured themselves with elbow locks on the landing skid, and finally climbed fully up on the skid as the Cobra continued its ascent from the rice paddy.

Flying carefully but steadily upward and away from the area, and still taking hits from the VC, Taylor was finally able to level off out of small arms range at 2,000 feet. He then turned south-west toward Saigon. After about 15 minutes of white-knuckle piloting, the Cobra-turned-troop-transport, with all the LRPs still aboard, landed carefully within the fenced confines of the Saigon Waterworks, near Tan Son Nhut Air Base. The team quickly jumped off, motioning their thanks to the Cobra crew via thumbs up and salutes, as Taylor lifted off to return to Phu Loi base.

Team Wildcat 2 were later picked up by a Huey 'slick' and taken to 1st Division headquarters at Dian, where they got hot showers and clean clothes, and were debriefed by G-2 officers. They were congratulated and told they had done an excellent job. Captain Taylor, whose Cobra had taken 16 hits while supporting the LRPs during the battle and subsequent extraction, received a Silver Star for his heroic actions that night. Elsner, Hill, and Cohn were each awarded the Silver Star, while Paddy received a Bronze Star with 'V' Device, for their actions. Thus occurred the first, and possibly the only, Cobra gunship extraction of the Vietnam War.

SERGEANT LAW'S SACRIFICE

On 1 February 1969, all personnel and assets of the unit, commanded by Captain Allen A. Lindman, were reorganized into I Company (Ranger), 75th Infantry. Operational control of this unit was initially under the 3rd (Iron) Brigade, but later passed to Division G-2 (Intelligence) for the duration. From 1 January 1969 until deactivation as part of Phase III withdrawal on 7 March 1970, I Company operated in areas that were primarily under night-control and often day-control of the enemy. During February, the first month of I Company, 52 missions were conducted beginning with six on the first day of operation. In the later months, fewer missions were conducted. The unit undertook a total of 372 classified tactical operations which resulted in 205 recorded sightings, and 191 engagements with the enemy.

Towards the end of February 1969, Team 3 was one of eight I Company teams inserted along the Song Be river-infiltration corridor and in the Long Nguyen Secret Zone, in Binh Duong Province, to monitor enemy reinforcement and supply lanes. Operating outside Fire Support Base Thunder II, an advanced division outpost near Highway 13, Team 3 were moving stealthily through the dense jungle towards the Song Be when point man Sp4 Michael Cannon heard faint coughing ahead. Simultaneously ATL Sp4 Daniel Wiggins heard movement in the undergrowth behind them and spotted an enemy soldier. Deciding his mission had been compromised, Team Leader Sp4 Raymond Cervantes Jr. hand-signalled his team to head rapidly to a pre-selected pick-up zone. Arriving at a marshy clearing by the Suoi Ong Bang, a tributary of the Song Be, Sp4 Robert D. Law covered the approaches, while the other Rangers planted claymore mines around the perimeter of the extraction site.

Within minutes a VC unit crept into view and Law, quickly joined by the rest of the team, opened fire with the purpose of keeping the enemy at bay until air support appeared overhead. The arriving helicopters strafed and rocketed the enemy positions, giving the Rangers the opportunity to detonate most of their claymores before slipping into the Suoi Ong Bang and wading quietly away from the danger zone. Radioing for extraction, the team was refused as they were no longer under fire, no one was hurt, and it was almost dark.

After a short rest, Team 3 continued moving down the stream until it reached an open tract of swampland, in the midst of which was a small footbridge. Reporting the structure, they were ordered to mount a surveillance operation at the location. The Rangers set up defensive positions and lay watching for about 24 hours. At 0800 hours on 22 February, they observed three VC soldiers approaching and opened fire. All three enemy soldiers fell wounded, but began throwing fragmentation and gas grenades at the Rangers, who were running short of ammunition.

Moving to the right flank of the team's position, Specialist Law began placing suppression fire on the VC, when he saw a grenade land near radio operator Bill Powell and Sp4 Robert Rossien. Instead of diving into the safety of the stream behind him, Law courageously threw himself on the grenade to save the lives of his comrades. The remaining Rangers went on to kill all three enemy soldiers, after which they searched their bodies, recovered some documents, and were successfully extracted out. Sp4 Robert D. Law was posthumously awarded the Congressional Medal of Honor for this selfless bravery by the Suoi Ong Bang in February 1969. As such, he was the first member of the 75th Infantry (Airborne) to receive this award.

HIGHLAND RANGERS

Officially designated K Company (Ranger), 75th Infantry on 1 February 1969, this unit began service in the high-mountain tropics of Pleiku and Kontum provinces during November 1966 as recondo patrols operating within the 4th Infantry Division. As a result of Operation 'Sam Houston' which began on New Year's Day, 1967, these embryonic units were expanded with one 62-man platoon attached to each brigade in the division. Each platoon was composed of a headquarters section, eight recondo teams made up of between three and eight soldiers, and three 'Hawkeye' teams.

The recondo teams, which also incuded an expert sharpshooter, served as specialized counter-measure units to eliminate enemy officers, couriers, or sentries. The Hawkeye teams, modelled on Special Forces-led native troops, and consisting of two division recondos with two indigenous warriors of the Rhade Montagnard tribe, conducted missions requiring native skills. Both team types became expert at hit-and-run ambushes and gathering battlefield intelligence, and in some instances they combined to lure the enemy into revealing his position. The most dangerous tactic involved a decoy Hawkeye team feigning patrol trouble. Enemy pursuit troops were drawn into an ambuscade and, if successful, a recondo team or sudden artillery bombardment, would destroy them while the Hawkeye unit escaped.

The brigade reconnaissance platoons were fully operational by the beginning of April 1967, and during that month began their commitment to Operation 'Francis Marion', which went on until October and did much to stifle NVA attempts to cross large forces over the border from Cambodia into Vietnam. During June, Major General William Peers supplemented the brigade reconnaissance platoons by forming the provisional 4th Infantry Division Recondo Detachment. Commanded and staffed as part of the intelligence section, and administratively assigned to the 1st Squadron, 10th Cavalry, this Detachment received helicopter support and back-up from

Opposite, **Team Hawkeye 1 Alpha, K Company (Ranger), 75th Infantry (Airborne), were on a mission north-west of Mang Yang Pass, when this photograph was taken on 22 February 1969. The Ranger on the left holding the taped-up CAR-15 is Emmett Mulroney. Team Leader Sergeant Wallate 'Ratman' Thibodeau** **stands at centre wearing Tigerstripes. Note his shoulder holster which held a .357 revolver. Matthew Gentilella stands at right. An excellent 'Tunnel Rat', Sergeant Thibodeau served four tours of duty in South Vietnam before being killed in action during a mission on 19 July 1969.** *Emmett Mulroney*

the aero rifle platoon of Troop D, 10th Cavalry.

From April through October 1967, the 4th Division Recondo-Hawkeye forces provided accurate surveillance reports which pinpointed the shifting locations of both the 1st and 10th NVA Divisions. They completed 555 missions that resulted in 366 sightings of enemy personnel. Engaging in 82 fire-fights, they killed 90 NVA/VC soldiers. During the following Operation 'MacArthur', they accomplished a further 698 missions and reported 411 enemy observations, earning themselves a reputation as one of the finest reconnaissance units in Vietnam.

On 20 December 1967, E Company (LRP), 58th Infantry, was activated using the personnel

Sergeant Thibodeau's Team spent the night in a bomb crater while on a mission to find two missing American soldiers during May, 1969. Top left is Emmett Mulroney while Matty Gentilella, to his right, has his M-16 with silencer by his side. Delmer Long is turning to the camera. A PRC-25 short-range FM radio in a rucksack lies in the foreground.
Emmett Mulroney

and assets of the 4th Division Infantry Recondo Detachment. After further training and despite being plagued by constant personnel turnover, the 'Echo 58th Patrollers' continued to operate in the rugged western mountains of Kontum Province during the summer and fall of 1968, conducting both long and short-range patrols. The value of loyal native expertise was demonstrated during this period on a trail-monitoring patrol east of Dak To led by Sergeant George Douglas. The four-man patrol included a Montagnard scout called Y-Truck.

Spotting a lone NVA soldier approaching along the trail, Sergeant Douglas was just about to let loose with his M16 when Y-Truck motioned him to hold fire. Puzzled, Douglas eased his finger off the trigger as 20 more enemy personnel began to appear, spaced at 20-foot intervals. Upon completion of their surveillance mission, the team began receiving hostile fire as it moved towards the pick-up point. Caught in an exposed position, Douglas had his weapon shot out of his hands and found himself looking momentarily down the wrong end of an AK-47, when Y-Truck again intervened and killed the enemy soldier. The team leader then picked up his fallen opponent's weapon and rejoined the fire fight. The team went on to kill the entire enemy pursuit squad, popped smoke grenades, and was shortly after picked up intact by the extraction helicopter.

K Company (Ranger), 75th Infantry, was initially activated under the command of Captain Reuben H. Silverling on 1 February 1969, using the existing assets and personnel of 'Echo 58th'. This unit continued to operate in the western Central Highlands from the northern An Lao valley of Kontum Province, across Pleiku and Darlac provinces, to Bu Krak in western Quang Duc Province. K Company did not operate at full efficiency until the three brigade LRRP platoons were finally integrated with the Ranger company on 6 October 1969, under the command of Captain Kim H. Olmstead. The three added platoons gave the company extra manpower and allowed it to reach its authorized strength of 220 members with a 53-man company headquarters and three patrol platoons. This unit was placed under operational control at division level, while assignment to the 1st Squadron, 10th Cavalry, continued. Each patrol platoon contained a headquarters section, five five-man Ranger teams, and five three- to six-man Hawkeye teams, one member of which was a native scout.

On 18 July 1969, Team Hawkeye 1 Alpha led by Sergeant Wallate 'Ratman' Thibodeau was inserted in 'Happy Valley' to seek out an NVA regiment which had attacked the division's base at Camp

Radcliffe near An Khe. Team member Emmett Mulroney recalled: 'Once found, we had to observe force size, types of weapons being carried, and direction of movement. On our second day out, we were on the move when we stopped in a bunch of rocks to take a break when a squad of NVA regulars came right toward us and engaged in small arms fire. We called in the gunships and after they had expended their load, "Rat" and Denny [Belonger] moved forward to check for enemy dead and were killed by the NVA.

'Everywhere we looked, Robert Thomas and I now saw NVA approaching us. I was wounded in the face by a grenade. We then ran to our LZ where Lt. Fillippini's personal command chopper flew in to rescue us. After we boarded, the chopper was shot down by a B-40 rocket which hit its rear end. Lt. Fillippini then took the M-60 machine gun from its mount and held off the NVA as he directed the gunships where to fire from a hand-held radio. The enemy then retreated and after two hours, the Air Force got us out with a McGuire Rig on a Husky Helicopter. Lt. Fillippini was shot in the leg and grazed on the forehead from a bullet and had a broken arm. One pilot and one door gunner were also shot, and I had a broken neck and back and everyone had something broken.'

EXTENDED MISSION

Warren Gallion served with the 2nd Brigade LRRPs, 4th Infantry Division from April until September 1969. Inserted with his team in the Central Highlands, to the south-west of Kontum, on 24 July, they endured an extended eight-day mission which stretched their training and resources to the limit. 'The mountain range formed a natural barrier between Vietnam and Laos,' he remembered. 'The mountains were steep and there was very little land that was suitable for farming. They were so high that helicopters had to fly through a pass rather than fly over them. They seem to go straight up on each side with a beautiful river waterfall cascading below. Clouds would often hang on top of the mountains and we would be given a triangular tunnel to pass through. My eyes told me I was seeing the Garden of Eden but my military experience reminded me of the danger of being channelled into such a narrow space.'

The mountains were also uninhabited, which gave the NVA some protection as they moved between North and South Vietnam. Much of the area had been designated as a free-drop zone where war planes could release bombs that, for one reason or another, did not get dropped over their designated targets. As they flew through the rugged valleys it was not unusual to see them scarred with bomb craters. A 500-pound bomb could make a crater 15 feet deep and over 30 feet across and leave no signs of the trees and earth that previously existed.

'With the exception of being startled by a monkey walking up on us, the mission had been uneventful', continued Gallion. 'On day 5, we were told that due to weather conditions, our extraction would be postponed. Knowing that we couldn't be extracted also meant it would be difficult to get gunship support if we needed it. We decided to quit moving and found a nice defensive position in some brush next to a bomb crater. The battery on our radio ran out and I installed the only back-up battery.

'On day 6, we were told to stand by, but the helicopters were still grounded. As we sat in the rain, it was obvious to us we would not be extracted. To conserve food, we decided to only eat one meal a day. On one of the radio checks, I was told there would be some heavy artillery in our area. It was not unusual for the artillery units to fire around us, so I acknowledged the information and turned the radio off. The rains had turned our camp into a mud pit. I tried to get as comfortable as I could while lying in the mud, hungry and trying to calculate how much longer the batteries might last before I lost contact with the world. The earth beneath me began to bounce me where I lay. Moments later, the noise reached my ears and the sound was deafening. I wondered if the whole earth was just crumbling apart. This Armageddon seemed to last an eternity but must have been less than a minute.

'I turned on the radio to see if the rest of the world survived this apparent disaster. I was relieved to hear a voice on the other end of the radio. I asked if they knew what had happened. "You must have heard the Arc Light [Multiple B-52s, dropping 500-pound bombs]. We were told you were more than three miles from the target area and would be OK, but we weren't permitted to broadcast the strike over the radio. We hoped you would understand the heavy artillery clue".

'On day 7 the rains stopped and things were looking up. We decided to conserve the battery on the radio, by doing radio checks every three hours instead of every two hours. To conserve food, we decided two men could share one ration for the day. We were told to stand by, but the helicopters were still grounded. I tried to visualize the pass being fogged over, but the blue skies and hot sun was making it difficult. As we dried out into mud cakes, we heard the sound of a helicopter. When I spotted the helicopter, I turned on the radio to see if this might be our extraction helicopter. Instead of my unit answering, another voice came over the radio. "Negative Delta Tango. This is Charlie Pappa, checking out the situation."

'I replied "This is Delta Tango, if this is not an extraction, don't waste my batteries!" and I turned off the radio. We could not believe that our spirits had been lifted only to be sunk again. The helicopter continued to fly in our area and the longer it flew, the madder we got. I turned on the radio again and said "This is Delta Tango, I have obviously spotted an enemy helicopter, since all of our birds are grounded. This helicopter says it can't come down, but if it flies over me one more time, I'll show you it can come down!" The helicopter left our area.

'Day 8, I would say a prayer each time I turned on the radio that the batteries still worked. We decided to postpone our half meal for the day until late afternoon. The day was cloudy and not nearly as clear as the previous day. We decided for Day 9 we would divide one meal four ways and we would do the same on Day 10 with our last meal. There was very little hope the radio would still be working on Day 10. I was already thinking about the survival skills I had been taught and about the increased danger in hunting for food. Our situation was becoming critical, but I knew we were not forgotten. I turned on the radio for an early afternoon check, and heard the only news I wanted to hear. "Get ready, the helicopters are already on their way."

'The helicopters were a beautiful sight as we popped smoke. The helicopter hovered over the bomb crater while we climbed aboard. We flew through the pass safely and watched from above as another LRRP team was extracted. When the helicopter landed, we were taken to the captain, our boots were still muddy from the field and we made tracks into his office. I'm not sure if the captain was more concerned about us or his office.'

After debriefing, the LRRPs were dismissed to get a meal and take a shower. As they marched out, the lieutenant informed them: 'The Battalion Commander, Colonel Pinney, wants YOU to know his call sign is "Charlie Pappa". "Yes Sir," responded Gallion, and the matter was never mentioned again!

AIRBORNE EAGLE RANGERS

The reconnaissance component of the 101st Airborne Division was organized during December 1965 when the 1st Brigade commander, Brigadier General James S. Timothy, authorized brigade headquarters to form its own long-range reconnaissance patrol platoon at Bear Cat-Bien. Each of the nine six-man teams had a leader, two scouts, a medical specialist, and two radiomen. Known as the 'Reconnaissance Nomads' because they operated across the length and breadth of South Vietnam, their first major operation, called 'Operation Harrison', involved night helicopter insertions into the Tuy Hoa sector in search of the 95th NVA Regiment. During the next few months, the paratrooper LRRPs participated in Operations 'Fillmore' and 'Austin' in Phu Yen Province, where they were backed up by infantry reaction companies. The latter involved the search for a VC redoubt astride the border between II and III Corps Tactical Zones. During one of these patrols, a team walked unexpectedly into an enemy training camp and surprised a class in session. After a short, bloody fire fight, the VC disappeared into the jungle, but the paratroopers managed to commandeer the lecture placards. Sent back to division intelligence for translation, they were found to read 'Beware of American Long Range Patrols'!

The Reconnaissance Nomads were next moved to Kontum Province where they took part in 'Operation Hawthorne'. Operating in the tri-border region near Cambodia, they located the 24th NVA Regiment entrenched in the mountains overlooking the Dak Tan Kan valley. This unit was subsequently destroyed by B-52 bombers and a heavy ground assault. Moved next to Phu Yen Province, the Reconnaissance Nomads patrolled endlessly through rainstorms and flooded mountain streams for the remainder of the year.

During 'Operation Summerall', which began during March 1967 in the central province of Khanh Hoa, a six-man Nomad patrol moving through heavy jungle in three two-man scouts teams made an important contact. Following a trail left by an enemy soldier, Sergeant Jimmy L. Cody and Sp5 Virgil D. Polk unexpectedly entered a clearing and surprised a small group of VC. The paratroopers immediately opened fire on full automatic, scattering what turned out to be a VC district command meeting. Pulling back and reconsolidating in an overnight position, the next day the Nomads guided an infantry reaction force to the site of their encounter. Searching the area,

they apprehended a VC suspect, who informed them that nine of the enemy soldiers had been killed by a 'two-man army'.

During July 1967, the Reconnaissance Nomad teams were absorbed into a unit nicknamed the 'Screaming Eagle Patrollers' (after the division patch worn by the 101st Airborne), and officially designated E Company (LRP), 20th Infantry (Airborne). This short-lived group was used as the nucleus for a field force patrol company within the 101st Airborne Division formed on 10 January 1968. Designated F Company (LRP), 58th Infantry (Airborne), the new unit consisted of parachute-trained volunteers commanded by Captain Peter

A radio telephone operator of an L Company team, 75th Infantry, moves cautiously through the jungle. The long antenna for his radio can be seen stuck down in his rucksack.
John Burford

Fitts. Under strength and lacking fully-trained recruits, this unit languished in defensive positions around Song Be, Bien Hoa, and Gia Le throughout the first half of 1968.

With each of its six-man teams supplemented by two scouts from the South Vietnamese 1st Division's *élite* 'Black Panther' strike company, F Company was again actively involved in reconnaissance work during May 1968. By October, the unit had been transferred from divisional intelligence staff control and became part of the air cavalry squadron. As such, it adopted a more active combat scouting role. During a patrol dubbed the 'Black November' mission

conducted on 19 November 1968, all 12 LRPs were either killed or wounded after an ambush operation went wrong.

By 13 February 1969, F Company, 58th Infantry, had been transformed into L Company (Ranger), 75th Infantry, and teams were designated after countries, cities, and automobiles. Integrated with the 2nd Squadron, 17th Cavalry, the unit operated solely in a divisional 'Reconnaissance Zone' which covered the western mountains and valleys adjacent to the Laotian border. As such they offered a buffer between enemy-held portions of Laos and the populated regions of coastal Vietnam.

Typical of missions conducted by L Company was

A Ranger team from the 75th Infantry (Airborne) moves rapidly into the tree line after insertion. The 'point man' has already disappeared in to the brush. This scene was photographed by a crewman on the backup Huey which monitored the men until they were safely under cover.
John Burford

the six-man team led by Sergeant Mike Vanning, which was inserted on 4 August 1970. Finding a booby trap and a well-used trail on the second day out, he requested an extension of his patrol box and moved parallel to the trail, setting up a point recon 10 feet from it. Within a short while, 23 NVA soldiers in pith helmets with AK47s and rucksacks slung with equipment passed within six feet of the patrol. Team member Bob Gilbert recalled: 'One of the NVA, about 35 to 40 years, did manage to stop directly in front of "Termite" (team member Mike Vanning,) to take a leak. I had my CAR-15 trained on his head. I was ready to trigger him when our eyes locked. He was dead meat and he knew it! Taking two steps backwards, the dink turned and faced his buddies. The other NVA kept looking in our direction and he kept hitting them on the shoulder, shoving them down the trail.

'Without lowering my weapon, I eased the patrol back down the mountain, took cover, listened, and the dead calm gave us a chance to move further away from the larger force. The radio was useless in the valley and I used the URC-10 to give a spot report to Hillsboro and informed them that I was hitting our E&E route since we were compromised. My mind was racing at the enemy's possible actions after being observed.

'Two pink teams from the 2nd Battalion, 17th Cavalry came on station and Lieutenant Brownsberger ordered us to be extracted through the triple canopy jungle. No time to get Stabo or McQuire rigs from Quang-Tri. It was going to be a Swiss seat extraction on rappelling ropes and we went out two at a time. Jim Suomela and Greg Weaver first, Ken Stiemel and Sergeant Hipwell, my assistant next. Almost dark now, I tied each man into his Swiss seat and put 12 overhand knots in each Ranger snap link and around it. Out of 327 Rangers in class six, only five failed the knot test. The knot I never got right was the end of the line bowline.

'After tying Wimmer in, I reached for my weapon and rucksack and couldn't find them in the dark. At this point with the gunship action going on and coming our way, I hadn't tied my own Swiss seat, thinking I wouldn't need that around me if I go smoking through the jungle alone. Tripping over the rucksack in the dark, I whipped up the worst Swiss seat ever tied and told the pilot to take off.

'As we ascended it was obvious my Swiss seat was a "D" for Ranger school, but good enough. Halfway up through the canopy the chopper hit a limb with a blade strike and they pulled pitch causing Wimmer and I to shoot straight up through the canopy. The pilot told me later we were taking groundfire and green tracers were ripping past his

On a mission near the A Shau Valley, in Thua Thien Province, during November 1968, Sergeant Thomas Brooks, Team 21, F Company (LRP), 58th Infantry (Airborne), moves cautiously along a stream in search of a suitable point to climb up the steep banks. His M16 rifle is fitted with an experimental sound suppressor.
John Burford

windshield. The jolt of hitting the canopy with our heavy rucksacks flipped Wimmer and I upside down and the pilot, having cleared the canopy floorboarded the Huey. I knew I was in trouble with the Swiss seat and Wimmer was laughing and swung over by me yelling "whee, whee," – actually enjoying himself! He didn't scare period. As the bird increased speed, the Swiss seat slipped between my knees and butt and was pulling over my left side. The pilot took the bird up high, four or five thousand feet and I felt the rope slipping about one inch every 30 seconds. The handset for my PRC-25 was trailing behind us and I reeled it in and hollered: "Hey up there!" The pilot said, "Good to hear everything is okay." "Okay hell, I'm falling out of this Swiss seat. Set us down or I'm going down myself." "Hang on, buddy, I'll put her down as quick as I can."

'During the next few minutes in the pitch dark, I cracked off 10 Hail Mary's and an equal Our Father's and thought, "I can't hold on any longer!" The light under the Huey came on and I saw the ground about 100 feet below us and Wimmer and I were swinging in a 40 foot arc. We began hitting brush and trees and finally crashed into the ground. My left leg was paralyzed, Bob Wimmer was fumbling with the ropes when the bellyman, ran over, chopped both ropes and dragged us into the Huey. With gunships blazing on both sides,

An Army photographer, accompanying Team 21, F Company (LRP), 58th Infantry, LRRP team on patrol in 1968, captures the moment when 'point man' Sp4 Taylor froze after hearing a suspicious noise in the jungle.
John Burford

we lifted off and it reminded me of a "Sergeant Rock" comic book scene. My leg was locked in place and an hour passed after a muscle relaxant shot was given before I could move it.

'As Wimmer and I were being extracted through the canopy earlier, two Cobra gunships were working the ridge over and raining destruction on both sides of us. The ridge we'd seen the dinks on was literally on fire. Once we were clear, the 175 Howitzers bombed the place all night. I've often wondered how many men died in that onslaught.'

REDCATCHER RANGERS

The 71st Infantry Detachment (Long Range Patrol), consisting of 61 volunteers chosen by Brigadier General Robert C. Forbes, was organised within the ranks of F Company, 51st Infantry, 199th Infantry Brigade, on 20 December 1967. Within a month, this group was fully operational within the Long Binh sector of Bien Hoa Province, north-east of Saigon.

With the conclusion of the Tet campaign by the end of May 1968, the 199th Infantry Brigade was relocated south-west of Saigon, into the extensive marshlands commonly called the 'Pineapple' plantation. This flat swampy region offered an ideal VC approach corridor to Saigon, and General William C. Westmoreland believed that the brigade's presence there would hamper this activity. The 71st (LRP) was based at 'Horseshoe Bend' and conducted regular patrols into the bomb-scarred elephant grass clearings, rice paddies, and groves of fruit thickets and nipa palm. For over a year the 'Lurps' watched scores of footbridges and causeways across the water-logged landscape. Recon teams also operated successfully from Navy patrol boats along the Song Vam Co Dong river, landing ambush parties along the reed-covered banks and mud flats.

On 1 February 1969, the 71st Infantry Detachment was reorganized as M Company (Ranger), 75th Infantry. This unit was paired with

Troop D, 17th Cavalry, which gave it a combat reconnaissance and surveillance capability. Organised into teams with alphabetical designations, M Company sometimes patrolled in two-man teams, although the six-man team was standard, and a 12-man heavy team was used for combat patrols.

During June 1969, the 199th Brigade moved to a new operational area north-east of Saigon and resettled at Fire Support Base Blackhorse in Long Khanh Province. There M Company teams found vast jungles and sparsely populated rubber plantations, and encountered two large, well-trained, and highly disciplined enemy organizations, the 274th VC and the 33rd NVA Regiments. This expanded reconnaissance campaign forced the Rangers to establish long distance communications. For example, in late March 1970, one team was placed on a remote mountain top and set up a radio relay point for two weeks. Operating in the gloomy rain forests north-east of Trang Bom, north of Dinh Quan, and along the heavily vegetated Lga Nga and Dong Nai rivers, the M Company patrols grappled with the enemy in a series of sharp clashes, and disrupted so many of their re-supply trails that the 274th Regiment was reduced to eating bananas and roots. The 33rd NVA withdrew altogether from Long Khanh Province, still being pursued by 'Redcatcher Ranger' patrols.

A fine example of the role performed by M Company is the long-range mission of Sergeant David Reeser's 'Bravo' Team into the jungle near the Dong Nai river during September 1969. On the second day out, this patrol discovered an enemy base camp and counted a dozen camouflaged bunkers. Moving about 300 yards away, Sergeant Reeser prepared to call in artillery, and ordered Sp4 Lou Garland to clamber up a high tree to observe marking rounds for artillery firing adjustment.

Suddenly, Garland slid down the tree trunk, jumped to the jungle floor, and ran over to his waiting team members to report he had seen at least 20 NVA soldiers heading swiftly in their direction. Hastily the Rangers rigged a claymore mine and took cover in the dense foliage. As the enemy came into view, the claymore was detonated directly in their faces, while Sp4 Garland scored a direct hit with a grenade from his M79. The surviving NVA fell back into the jungle. Setting up machine guns, they began manoeuvring to surround the Ranger position.

Assimilating the situation, Sergeant Reeser radioed for air support, and F-100 fighter-bombers plus OV-10 Bronco observation aircraft, soon appeared overhead. Reeser tossed smoke grenades, and once identification had been confirmed, directed the Bronco forward air controllers via radio. Flying close to the tree tops despite heavy enemy fire, the Broncos reported enemy reinforcements rushing toward the fire fight. In a series of co-ordinated air assaults,

Sp4 Taylor crosses the third stream in as many days! He wears Tigerstripe boonie hat and jungle fatigues. The fore grip on his M16 is well camouflaged with OD tape. Note the 'Aircrew Survival Knife' taped to the harness on his webgear.
John Burford

the F-100s unleashed their 500-pound bombs while Cobra gunships rocketed the surrounding jungle, effectively blocking the path of the oncoming enemy.

The engagement between the 'Cobra' Team and the NVA platoon dragged on, with Reeser using up all available smoke grenades to contact aircraft on firing passes. He then set out an orange panel to signal their location to the gunships. Meanwhile, Ranger Specialist Arrell managed to spot and kill an enemy soldier who was slithering towards them with a bag filled with grenades. With their ammunition running low, the Rangers radioed for more and a fresh case of M16 magazines was bravely dropped in from a light observation helicopter. Eventually, after about three hours of intense action, combining determined infantry resistance and fierce aerial support, the NVA were forced to retire, and the Rangers were extracted without loss or casualties.

NOVEMBER RANGERS

The Long Range Reconnaissance Patrol Platoon, 173rd Airborne Brigade, was organized on 25 April 1966. Raised among the the 1st and 2nd Battalions of the 503rd Infantry, this unit supplemented Troop E, 17th Cavalry. Training was given to the LRRPs by the 1st Royal Australian Regiment who were familiar with jungle operations and were veterans of combat operations in Malaysia. Each of the nine six-man patrol teams was named after a predatory fish species, such as 'Shark', 'Bass', or 'Barracuda', while recon teams were given female names. This unit performed important service from the summer of 1966 through the fall of 1967, gaining invaluable intelligence about enemy infiltration routes, and performing tunnel searching and ambush patrols.

The 74th Infantry Detachment (Airborne LRP) was authorized on 20 December 1967, and all personnel of the LRRP platoon were absorbed into this unit. Involved in 'Operation Cochise',

a prolonged counter-insurgency campaign in northern Binh Dinh Province, the unit became known as the 'Cochise Raiders'.

On 19 October 1968, a team led by Sergeant Peter G. Mossman was located in the An Lao Valley, 20 miles north of Bong Son, when it was caught in one of the heavy storms resulting from the many typhoons which plagued that part of the South Vietnamese coast. Making contact with the enemy, despite the squalling wind and rain, they killed three VC and then found themselves being chased by a much larger force led by dogs. Pursued for over three hours, and unable to call in air support because of the weather and terrain, the exhausted team eventually managed to scale the crest of a ridge from where they could at last relay news of their predicament to elements of the Americal Division.

Despite the atrocious conditions, the commanding officer of the 61st Aviation Company sent out helicopters to rescue the men, who were instructed to head for an open area about 500 yards distant. Sergeant Mossman recalled: 'When we got to the pick-up zone, the NVA were practically breathing down our necks. They couldn't see us, though, because the visibility was down to about 25 metres. We couldn't see the choppers, either, but we could hear them, so we just kept signalling

Sp4s Burford and Taylor, F Company (LRP), 58th Infantry, cross yet another stream while on patrol.
John Burford

Opposite, **Sergeant Brooks, Team 21, F Company (LRP), 58th Infantry, helps radio telephone operator Sp4 Harris up a steep hill during a mission in 1968. Harris has a two-quart bladder type canteen on the back of his pistol belt, and a knife strapped to his leg.**
John Burford

with a strobe light and just hoped.'

Eventually one of the utility Hueys, piloted by Warrant Officer Sam Kyle, managed to spot the strobe after circling dangerously low over the elephant grass below. Looming down through the misty rain, Kyle fought to keep his aircraft steady as the LRPs clambered quickly aboard, and were whisked safely off.

LASZLO RABEL'S BRAVERY

On 13 November 1968, reconnaissance team 'Delta', led by Staff Sergeant Laszlo Rabel, was manning a patrol base on Hill 819 overlooking the Nuoi Luong river, when their position was suddenly compromised. Scout Pfc Arthur Bell heard sounds of enemy movement and glanced towards Sergeant Cameron T. McAllister, who nodded as they both aimed their M16s towards the noise. Radio Operator Sp4 Paul Desmond was on a rest break under a poncho with his PRC-25 handset held by his ear, when he was shaken by Sp4 Stephen Fryer, who whispered hoarsely: 'Movement to the front! Stay quiet!'

A strange silence descended over the jungle. Sergeant McAllister quietly asked if anyone could see anything, and Fryer held up one finger and whispered: 'I think he went back down.'

A few more seconds passed, and Staff Sergeant

Rabel and McAllister decided to check out the steep jungle-covered cliff side to their immediate front. Rabel rose to his feet and was stooping under a tree limb in preparation to lower himself down the steep slope, when a grenade bounced into their midst and struck a rock. Although the rest of the team had no time to react, Rabel threw himself on the grenade, and absorbed the full blast, thereby saving his team from death or injury. Mortally wounded, he rolled down the hillside. The other four team members fired claymore mines to hold off the lurking enemy, retrieved the fallen sergeant's body, and reached their pickup point from where they were extracted without further casualties. Staff Sergeant Laszlo Rabel, 74th Infantry Detachment (LRP) was awarded the Medal of Honor for his actions on Hill 819.

At the beginning of February 1969, the 74th Infantry Detachment was reorganized under Captain Richard D. James as N Company, 75th Infantry (Airborne). This unit consisted of three officers and 72 enlisted personnel. Twelve operational teams of six men each were composed entirely of enlisted personnel. Missions for the Ranger company were typically three to five days with a two-day break in between for debriefing, rest and preparation for the next mission. The Rangers continued to operate in the mountainous terrain of the An Lao, An Do, Suoi Ca, Crow's Foot valleys; the Highland Fishhook; and Nui Ba and Tiger Mountains of northern Binh Dinh province which bordered the I Corps area.

The 173rd Airborne Brigade Tet-69 campaign lasted from 9 February to 26 March 1969 and marked the first independent employment of a Ranger company in screening operations of the Vietnam War. During this typical period of Ranger operations, N Company conducted over 100 long range patrols that resulted in 134 sightings of enemy personnel and 63 enemy killed by direct action, five prisoners and a much larger number of enemy killed by Ranger-sponsored indirect fire and

P Company (Ranger), 75th Infantry, 1st Brigade., 5th Infantry Division (Mechanized) company sign. Camp Carter was named after Sfc David E. Carter, KIA on 10 August 1969.
Terry Roderick

Lima Rangers Team 1-1 in elephant grass near Khe Sanh. Ronnie Edwards is on the PRC-25 in the foreground.
Ron Edwards

reaction elements. The Rangers casualties for this period was one killed in action, 20 wounded and none captured or missing.

Typical of the eventful missions conducted by N Company patrols during this period was that of 'Team Juliet' on 21 February 1969. Having located an enemy base camp built into the caverns of a rocky overhang, they killed an enemy soldier who stumbled on them, and then withdrew and called in aerial bombardment. Re-entering the shattered complex later, they found numerous deserted 'spider holes' and underground bunkers, all of which had proved impervious to air strikes. They also discovered documents and weapons, which they gathered up, and then prepared for extraction.

The helicopter lift-out was hampered by incessant rain which caused one team member to fall from the slippery skids of the first extraction chopper. After a 15-minute search, a second aircraft located the fallen man on the thickly forested slope and hauled him safely aboard. Meanwhile, the patrol leader had remained on the ground to search for his fallen comrade, unaware that the injured man had been retrieved. Searching through the undergrowth, he stumbled upon two NVA soldiers and cut them down with his M16 as they attempted to give chase. Finally informed of the situation, the sergeant found a clearing and, using a cut-down emergency panel to signal a forward observation aircraft, was eventually rescued by helicopter.

ALL-AMERICAN RANGERS

The catalyst for O Company, 75th Infantry was a combination of reconnaissance units of the 3rd Brigade, 82nd Airborne Division (Separate), which were formed by Colonel Alexander Bolling Jr. in the mountainous Hue-Phu Bai region of northern South Vietnam in response to the Tet Offensive of 1968. During late October of that year, the 3rd Brigade relocated to the Saigon area, where the 78th Infantry Detachment (Airborne LRP)

was activated under Lieutenant William E. Jones. Stationed at Camp Red Ball, north-east of the capital, this unit conducted foot patrols amidst the muddy rice paddy fields.

Scouting along the banks of the Nha Be river, one patrol searched a nearby village and found a 50-year old Vietnamese woman in possession of documents listing details on most officers and NCOs assigned to MACV headquarters. Another night time patrol in the same area spotted a large amount of flotsam drifting slowly down the river. Ever suspicious, they fired machine guns and grenade launchers into it, and suddenly an M79 grenade round caused a tremendous explosion, followed by a series of secondary blasts. The LRPs had discovered and destroyed a heavily camouflaged VC ammunition resupply vessel.

With the re-creation of the 75th Infantry on 1 February 1969, the 78th Infantry Detachment was deactivated and its members were absorbed into O Company (Ranger). Fully operational by

A Papa Company Ranger Team leaves for a five-day mission in the Demilitarized Zone in 1970.
Terry Roderick

1 March 1969, this unit patrolled the outer Saigon area throughout that summer, following which they were deployed as part of Operation 'Yorktown Victor' in the Iron Triangle. In the southern Phu Hoa district, the unit was frequently employed as stay-behind forces. On one occasion, less than an hour after the line company was extracted from the area, a team captured two VC who provided valuable intelligence concerning enemy operations in the area.

On 20 November 1969, O Company was officially deactivated prior to the departure of the 3rd Brigade from Vietnam, but was reactivated at Fort Richardson, Alaska, on 4 August 1970 as the 'Arctic Rangers', in order to provide a strike force to protect the oil fields discovered at Prudhoe Bay.

RED DEVIL RANGERS

The 1st Brigade, 5th Infantry Division (Mechanised), from which P Company (Ranger),

Two Lima Rangers teams set off in defiant mood for a truck insertion from their company area at Camp Eagle outside Phu Bai. Note the rear vehicle bears the designation '101 AB 75 INF – RGR 11'.
Ron Edwards

75th Infantry, evolved was the last major US combat unit to fight in Vietnam. Arriving at Quang Tri Province, the northernmost area of I Corps, during July 1968, the 1st Brigade was supported by armoured personnel carriers, tanks, and other assorted motorized transport. Nicknamed the 'Red Devil Brigade', the unit was based at Camp 'Red Devil', and was assigned a large sector of responsibility along the Demilitarized Zone between North and South Vietnam, which stretched from the Gulf of Tonkin in the east to the Laotian border in the west.

The Red Devil Brigade performed search-and-clear expeditions on the Khe Sahn Plains, secured Highway 9 to the Laotian border, and disrupted enemy use of Highway 926. It also guarded the region's rice harvest and agriculturally rich coast line. Despite such heavy responsibilities, the brigade was not authorised a separate reconnaissance and ground-patrolling capabalility until 15 December 1968, when the 79th Infantry Detachment (LRP) was activated. This unit was still training when it was supplemented by personnel transferred up north from F Company (LRP), 51st Infantry, II Field Force, who had been replaced by the Indiana Rangers. Converted to brigade-level status, F Company was absorbed into P Company, 75th Infantry, on 1 February, and the regiment of Rangers was complete. This unit averaged about 26 six-man missions per month. Most teams were inserted and extracted via helicopter, although about 15 per cent of all patrols took advantage of brigade assets and were deployed in either armoured personnel carriers or tanks.

In May 1969, a patrol led by Sp4 Tom Snow had been inserted but a few hours, when they observed several North Vietnamese scouts setting up an observation post. 'We knew they were setting up overnight in the bunker to conduct sightings the next day', Snow recalled. 'They were recon NVA. They were at the ready, and knew what they were doing, watching every inch of the ground.' Monitoring the enemy intently until they disappeared back into the jungle, the Rangers hastily set up heavily camouflaged claymore mines around the bunker in anticipation that the scouts might drop their guard on their return. As predicted, the NVA relaxed their vigilance as they came back, and the Rangers detonated their mines, killing both men. Important documents, letters, and wallets, were taken from the bodies before the Rangers made off to their extraction zone.

Each P Company team included a trained sniper, but because of terrain and mission objectives, they were seldom used operationally. However, one of their most successful missions involved the assassination of communist guerrilla leader Nguyen Quyet in June 1969. The Intelligence Collection Division of XXIV Corps rated Quyet as 'the most wanted Viet Cong guerrilla leader in Quang Tri Province', and the Special Forces had been trying to kill him for about six years without success. A heavy sniper team was inserted along a ridge overlooking the Ba Long Valley, eight miles southwest of Quang Tri. Establishing an observation post, they settled down and waited.

The senior sniper remembered: 'I saw movement in the trees and then saw a man walking briskly down the creek bank toward the east. He was carrying an M16 rifle and was walking hunched over with his cap pulled low on his head and his collar turned up. I stayed down and waited until he was about 20 metres away and then I opened fire.' The Ranger struck his target. A missing little finger subsequently confirmed the identity of the dead man as Nguyen Quyet. Previously undefeated, his leaderless guerrilla band now effectively ceased operations in Quang Tri Province.

With the de-escalation of US commitment to the war in Vietnam, the major combat organizations were withdrawn along with their assigned Ranger units. Many of these divisions and brigades were stood down and removed from the active rolls of the army. The outfits which did return Stateside reverted back to a peacetime status which did not require a reconnaissance capability. The war was not won and the conflict remained unresolved, but the 'men with painted faces' had done their best.

By June 1972, only one US recon unit remained in South Vietnam – H Company of the 1st Cavalry Division. Gradually reduced in strength, this unit could only field five teams by that time. The last enemy soldier fell to the Rangers on 21 June 1972, when Team 7-1 of H Company, led by Staff Sergeant Clifford Price, ambushed four NVA in the Xa Gian Kiem area, killing one man and recovering his weapon, ammunition, pack, plus some documents.

The last US Ranger mission of the Vietnam War took place on 16 July 1972, when seven men of Team 7-2 under Corporal John E. Roessler conducted a patrol in the Tan Uyen region in support of the 1st Cavalry Division's Task Force 'Garry Owen'. It is doubtful whether team member Sergeant James Rogers had time to reflect on the association of his name with the colonial Rangers of Robert Rogers. On 15 August 1972, H Company, 75th Infantry (Airborne) was finally stood down, and the proud service of the Ranger in Vietnam drew to a close.

Terry B. 'Rock' Roderick, M-79 grenadier, of Killer 1-5, P Company, on the Old French Trail, just off the Ben Hai River, Demilitarized Zone, Vietnam 1970.
Terry Roderick

ARMING
THE RANGER

As a special force, the Rangers and LRPs of the Vietnam War were given a great deal of freedom in the choice of uniform, weapons, and individual equipment they used. What a man wore, fought with, and carried on missions and patrols was dependent not on regulation or tradition but quite simply on what the team leader, with the help of his assistant, considered was essential for a particular assignment.

The development of the Army's standard field uniform since the involvement of US troops in Vietnam had an obvious bearing on clothing the Rangers wore between 1969 and 1972. The Olive Green 107 (OG-107) Utility Uniform, or 'fatigues', had given way in 1963 to a new Tropical Combat Uniform of the same colour. Indeed, Special Forces, pathfinders, and scout dog teams were the first US personnel to receive this clothing.

Patterned after the Second World War parachutist's outfit, the generously cut suit of cotton-poplin offered some protection against insects and other jungle hazards, besides being relatively cool and quick-drying. Designed to be worn outside the trousers, the six-button 'coat' had a full length gas-flap down the inside of the front, which could be buttoned across the throat. Each of the four pockets were flapped and secured by two exposed buttons. The two chest pockets were slanted at an angle towards the gas-flap, and had a 'bellows' gusset in the inside edge and bottom, while the two hip pockets were horizontal with 'bellows' gussets in both sides and the bottom. The first-pattern coat also had epaulettes and side-tightening straps at the waist. The trousers had thigh cargo pockets incorporating integral tie-down tapes which were secured around the thighs in order to keep loose trouser legs from snagging on thorns or vines.

A modified second-pattern coat of the same material was produced during 1965-67. To overcome the problem of snagging in the jungle undergrowth, the pocket buttons were concealed under the flaps. The third-pattern cotton-poplin coat omitted the shoulder and waist straps for the same reason, and retained the concealed pocket buttons. Prone to ripping in the damp vegetation of the Vietnamese jungles, the poplin material was replaced in 1968 with reinforced 'rip-stop' cotton clothing incorporating a nylon weave which proved more durable.

Although the Tropical Combat Uniform was worn by most US soldiers during the Vietnam conflict, it offered insufficient camouflage for a reconnaissance team which survived on blending in with the environment. Prior to the major deployment of troops in Vietnam, the wearing of camouflage went very much against the doctrine of the US Army, which held that camouflage was defensive, even passive, in nature while the philosophy behind all tactics and training was purely offensive. Hence, camouflage uniforms were not even available for issue in the Army inventory at the time.

TIGERSTRIPE

By late 1967, reconnaissance-type troops began to receive the US Army's new camouflage uniform. Identical in cut to the third-pattern, olive green, Tropical Combat Uniform, it bore a four-colour, random leaf pattern first developed in 1948 by the Army's Engineer Research Development Laboratories. Subsequently known as ERDL, which some Rangers called 'tree-camouflage', this clothing was widely available by the time the Rangers of the 75th Infantry (Airborne) were formed in 1969. As with the Tropical Combat Uniform, ERDL jungle fatigues were originally produced in 1967 in less durable cotton-poplin, but were replaced during the following year by the 'rip-stop' version. When first issued, they were made in lime green-dominant 'Lowland' camouflage, but by 1969 the light brown dominant 'Highland' pattern was also available.

All forms of the Army's ERDL-patterned

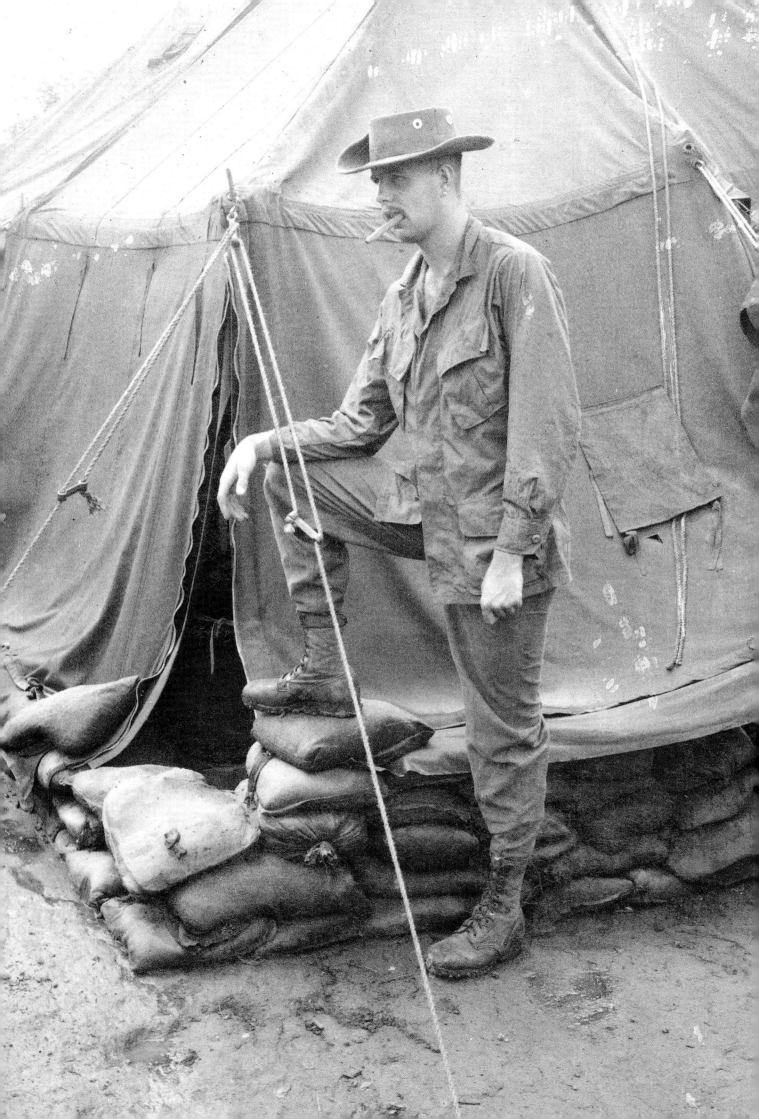

uniforms, which some men also affectionately referred to as 'Flower Powers', quickly gained high acceptability, despite problems with the cotton poplin. The material was lighter and much more comfortable than indigenous clothing, while the leaf-pattern camouflage was more effective in resisting infra-red and other thermal imaging detection methods employed by NVA snipers.

Not all Rangers wore 'trees' around the company area or base camp. According to Jim Zwiebel, K Company, 75th Infantry: 'After you pulled five missions or had made contact you could wear the tree fatigues all the time – or after 10 missions or a contact you could wear leopard or tiger fatigues. This was just an unwritten rule in our platoon. If someone was wearing trees in our base camp that we didn't know, we would ask them why, in a manner of speaking because we all earned our right to wear them.'

The development of Tigerstripe camouflage began in the early 1960s, when the Civilian Irregular Defense Group (CIDG) programme, sponsored by the CIA in order to enlist ethnic, political, and religious minorities in Vietnam, had made available to US Army Special Force advisers what it could in the way of camouflage clothing. With its green-and-black spots on a khaki background, the 'Duck Hunter', or 'Leopard', camouflage pattern dated back to Korea and the Second World War.

Initially, the CIDG purchased 'Duck Hunter' shirts and trousers off the shelf from the likes of Sears Roebuck. Meanwhile, in August 1959 the Vietnamese Marine Corps had adopted for combat duty a distinctive 'Sea Wave' pattern uniform, later known as 'Tigerstripe', which many US specialists and advisers also acquired and began to wear. Descended from the French 'lizard' camouflage worn by the French and colonial airborne forces during their involvement in Indo-China during the early 1950s, it was patterned with black stripes against an olive green background.

With the expansion of their programme, and greater military funding via the Mutual Defense Assistance Programme (MDAP), the CIDG let formal contracts in several south-east Asian countries for uniforms basically cut in the same American style but available in two main types of camouflage – 'Duck Hunter', and 'Tigerstripe'.

These MDAP-funded uniforms were made in Okinawa, Thailand, and Korea, being produced in both Vietnamese and American sizes, labelled A-S, A-M, A-L, and A-XL for 'Asian Small, Medium, Large, and Extra Large', and U.S.-M and U.S.-L for Americans. The six-button shirt had two flapped chest pockets and came with or without shoulder straps. Gradually the 'Tigerstripe' pattern, which proved surprisingly effective in the lush and verdant regions of Vietnam's disputed jungles and forests, became more popular and MDAP-sponsored production shifted mainly into this line.

The Vietnamese Marine pattern shirt was made of lightweight cloth, had two flapped patch pockets which fastened with a single green four-hole button, and plain cuffs. The shoulders were reinforced front and rear with a curved seam, a characteristic of other Vietnamese-made uniforms. The Tigerstripe patterning used was quite distinctive, containing a high proportion of light green which gave it a rather murky appearance.

The shirt produced via MDAP funding was without reinforced shoulders, and had buttoned cuff bands. The chest pockets on the Vietnamese version of this pattern incorporated a 'bellows' gusset in only one vertical edge, the other being sewn down. Referred to as 'chicken' pockets by Vietnamese tailors, the derivation of this name is unknown. Various types of buttons were attached to these shirts, including US-supplied Army brown plastic buttons; locally procured green, black, or blue buttons; and even late 1960s US Army oval-section buttons.

Other MDAP pattern shirts, tentatively identified as having been made via contract in Korea, were of

From top to bottom, **Shoulder patches worn by the Long Range Reconnaissance Patrols, or LRRPs, of E Company, 52nd Infantry. The Air Cavalry and divisional patches beneath indicate that this unit belonged to the 1st Cavalry Division. Below these are shoulder scroll patches worn by various Ranger companies of the 75th Infantry (Airborne) from 1969** through 1972 (top to bottom): E and H Companies are both of Vietnamese manufacture – note the scroll ends on the former are not forked, while the latter is a rare version showing division status rather than the usual 75th Infantry designation; M and O Companies were both made in Okinawa; the subdued L Company scroll is of US manufacture. *Author/Alex Allen and Neil Holdom*

heavyweight cloth, and had distinctive 'chicken' pockets with 'bellows' seam, usually on the inside edge only, and buttons concealed under the flaps. This latter feature overcame the problem of buttons being torn off by snagging on brush in the field.

The 'Vietnamese Marine' pattern trousers resembled the US OG-107 fatigue trousers. Of lightweight cloth, they had both front and rear patch pockets, the latter being secured by exposed-button flaps. Six 2½ in. long belt loops were attached to the waist band. An additional feature, not found on other patterns, was a reinforcing patch on each knee.

Trousers produced via MDAP sources were made from heavyweight cloth and had seven pockets consisting of two front, two rear, and two side, with the addition of a small pocket for a field dressing, or cigarettes, on the left leg only. All except the front pockets were closed by exposed-button flaps with either one or two buttons. Later versions of this pattern were produced without the front pockets which were, in any case, inaccessible when wearing webbing gear.

Another Tigerstripe camouflage pattern which became available was that worn by the Army of the Republic of Vietnam (ARVN) Rangers. Formed during the expansion of the Vietnamese Army in the mid-1960s by drawing one company from each infantry battalion and grouping them together into special battalions, the Vietnamese Rangers were treated as an *élite* force and given their own camouflage uniform. Made by Quartermaster Directorate contracts in Vietnam, the ARVN Ranger shirt could be manufactured from either lightweight or heavyweight cloth. They had plain cuffs and large, flapped 'chicken' pockets closed by two buttons each. Widely copied by tailor shops in both Vietnam and the US, individuals often requested small modifications, such as an extra pocket on the sleeve. ARVN Ranger pattern trousers usually had the same

The predominantly lime-dominant, Lowland ERDL jungle fatigues based on the third-pattern, olive-green Tropical Combat Uniform, was first introduced in cotton poplin during late 1967. The reconstruction shows the later rip-stop version available from 1968 through 1972.

Note the six-button front is covered by a flap, while further flaps conceal the two buttons on the each of the sloping chest pockets. This feature prevented the buttons from snagging on jungle undergrowth.
Author/Alex Allen and Neil Holdom

combination of pockets as early-version MDAP trousers, minus the 'field dressing' pocket on the left leg. Some Vietnamese tailors added 'bellows' to the side pockets in emulation of the cargo pockets found on US jungle fatigues. A much wider variety of Tigerstripe clothing became available in Vietnam after the arrival of greater numbers of US troops in 1965. Items included hats, berets, survival vests, flight suits, and even swimming costumes.

According to Daniel Pope of 'Charlie Rangers': 'Tiger fatigues could be had by trading, usually with US Army Special Forces. Tiger stripes were standard issue for them. I went from an SF "A" Team to Co E (LRP) and wore my Tigers until they fell apart and then had to resort to the green "trees" uniform.' Not all Rangers took to Tigerstripe clothing. Bob Crawford, 4th Infantry Division LRRPs, recalled: 'The Tiger fatigues just didn't fit my 6 ft. 2in.,160 lb body. I had one pair of Tigerstripe fatigues that were Asian XL – way too small, the pants legs came to about the top of my boots. The shirt was small and too tight to wear.'

Whichever camouflage clothing the Ranger wore, his uniform was mostly 'sanitized' for operational purposes. Unit patches, rank insignia, or name tapes were not always worn on long range insertions, thereby preserving camouflage and denying the enemy information about the unit involved.

Some Rangers also wore black indigenous or dyed US combat clothing in order to blend in during night operations, or to confuse the enemy from a distance.

Certain teams dressed all members in captured enemy apparel, which were usually carried into action and donned after insertion at the reconnaisance zone. 'Kurtz, Barretto, and I wore them or a combination of black and regular camouflage on at least four missions', recalled David Ham, 2nd Brigade 'Lurps', 4th Infantry Division, 'I don't remember whose idea it was, but we decided to try a three-man team and wear

black fatigues. Someone knew a Special Forces guy in the Special Operations Group in Kontum. One day we met him and traded a couple of M-16 flash suppressors for three sets of black uniforms. They were good quality and had no writing of any kind on them. I remember next going to the SOG bar in Kontum and trading an additional six flash suppressors for more fatigues, and some black floppy hats – which I loved! We were extremely careful when choppers came to pick us up because we were afraid that they would think we were gooks and open up. On one of our missions in the Plei Trap valley we… told them 300 times that when we came out of the wood line we would be in black fatigues. When we walked out, we heard a big commotion. One guy was real upset and said he almost shot us because he thought we were gooks. I think we quit wearing the fatigues after that.'

Japanese-American Rangers had particular problems when dressed in enemy uniforms. Sergeant Ted Yoshimura, H Company, 75th Infantry, recalled: 'I wore NVA web gear and carried an AK47 to confuse the enemy and give my team that split second we may have needed to get a jump on them.' A 'Charlie Troop' helicopter pilot, 1/9 Helicopter Assault Squadron, who extracted Sergeant Yoshimura's team later remembered telling his crew: 'Don't shoot the NVA approaching the helicopter, he's one of ours!'

Things were very different back in company area and base camp, where men were fully badged-up in their jungle fatigue and olive green Tropical Combat profile uniforms. On the first-pattern Tropical Combat Uniform ,a gold embroidered-on-black silk 'U.S. ARMY' tape was worn sewn horizontally above the left chest pocket, while a black-on-white name tape was attached in the same position above the right chest pocket. From 1966, the LRRPs wore various unofficial shoulder arcs and parent unit patches on their sleeves. With the re-designation of the 75th Infantry in 1969, all 15 Ranger companies

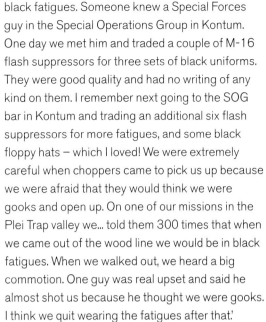

Developed by the US Army's Engineer Research Development Laboratories in 1948, ERDL camouflage jungle fatigues were widely used by the LRPs and Rangers. The lime-dominant Lowland version was more suited to the lush jungles and grasslands, while the brown-dominant Highland pattern was ideal for operations in the less verdant highlands of Vietnam.
Author/Alex Allen and Neil Holdom

Lime-dominant, Lowland jungle fatigue trousers made from rip-stop ERDL. Note the adjustable strap either side of the rear waist. Although this pair has a zip fly, many pairs of jungle fatigue trousers were made with button flys.
Author/Alex Allen and Neil Holdom

adopted an unauthorized, full-colour Ranger company scroll which was worn above the shoulder sleeve insignia patch at the top of the left sleeve. The former showed the regimental and company designation, and the latter indicated the army, corps, field force, division, or brigade to which the soldier was attached. Subdued variation black-on-green twill patches, name tapes, and rank insignia were authorized on 9 June 1966, but the Rangers often chose to continue wearing their full colour patches as a matter of pride.

Small 'jump wings', and Combat Infantryman's patches were often sewn or pinned to the front of the coat. In September 1969, a directive ordered the 'US ARMY' and name tapes sewn parallel to the top of the slanting pockets. Officers' rank insignia was worn on the right collar of the jungle fatigues, while the branch service insignia consisting of crossed muskets was sewn or pinned to the left collar. Non-commissioned officers' and enlisted men's chevrons were usually worn on both sleeves, but were sometimes pinned to their turned down collar instead.

BERETS AND BOONIE HATS

Modern Rangers first used the beret during the Korean War while undergoing training at Fort Benning. Remarkably similar in style to the Scottish cap or tam-o'-shanter, worn by many of Rogers' Rangers in 1756, the black beret was unofficially adopted by some LRP units before their reorganization in February 1969. Hence, when they were formed into the 75th Infantry (Airborne), this headwear continued to be worn on a limited basis in base camp and garrison, although it was not officially recognised as such until 20 December 1978. As there were no regulations for wearing insignia on the beret, many variations appeared. Some units sported locally embroidered flashes in various shield-shapes representing the Distinctive Insignia or crest of the regiment, which in turn was derived from the Second World War Merrill's Marauders patch. This was also worn in the form of a small enamelled metal crest, above which either jump wings or a company scroll might be pinned.

On missions and patrols, Rangers preferred various types of 'soft cover' rather than the issue M1 Helmet, or 'steel pot', commonly worn by the Army and Marine Corps. The helmet was too noisy, cumbersome, and distinctive for reconnaissance work. Most Rangers preferred the 'Hat, Jungle w/Insect Net', or 'Boonie', with its low crown and semi-rigid brim which could be shaped and moulded, resulting in a great variety of styles and uses. Modelled on the Field Hat worn by the US Army for fatigue wear since the First World War, it offered protection from the elements, and could be folded, carried in a pocket, or used as a pad in order to hold the barrel of a hot weapon. The first-pattern, OG 107 Boonie hat was issued in 1966, and had an adjustable chin cord, nylon foliage

Cambodian-pattern Tigerstripe in dark colours and a heavyweight cloth, with the 'cigarette' pocket on the left leg.
Author/Alex Allen and Neil Holdom

Vietnamese tailor shop-made copy in the so-called ARVN ranger pattern in a lightweight cloth. Note the chest pockets were fastened by exposed buttons.
Author/Alex Allen and Neil Holdom

loops, and two ventilation eyelets either side of the crown. As with coats and trousers, it was initially manufactured in cotton-poplin, being replaced later by a more durable rip-stop fabric version. The separate insect net issued with this headgear was seldom worn. By 1967, the ERDL camouflage version of the Boonie was available, minus insect net. Locally-produced hats manufactured in all the variations of ERDL and Tigerstripe camouflage patterns and weights of fabric, and usually minus the chin cord and insect net, were also available by that time.

K Company (Ranger), 75th Infantry, was sometimes referred to as 'Kangaroo Company' because they wore Australian bush hats. Jim Zwiebel recalled: 'When we were in base camp, we wore tree-camouflage safari hats with one side snapped up, and a black band that had K/75 embroidered in gold on it. I also had a string of blue beads, and a Combat Infantry Badge on mine. The First Sergeant would tell me to get rid of them, but I never did!'

Another form of Ranger headgear was the olive drab Utility Cap, first issued in 1962 to replace the field cap. Styled on the civilian baseball cap, its long soft bill and unflattering and non-military appearance was disliked by many men. Sometimes blackened metal rank insignia, unit-specific crests

or subdued patches were pinned or sewn to these hats and caps, especially when badged-up in camp. Grenade ring-pulls were often attached to the foliage loops of the Boonies, while names, peace-signs, and slogans such as 'Kill Congs', 'Don't Shoot Me, I'm Short' and worse were sometimes inked or embroidered on headgear. Others wore camouflage helmet covers fashioned into berets. According to Bob Crawford, 4th Infantry Division LRRPs: 'We wore a soft jungle hat, the hat always went inside the shirt on insertions or extractions, so you didn't lose it to rotor blast.'

Many LRPs and Rangers preferred no hat at all. They preferred a triangular, olive drab piece of cotton bandage taken from the first aid kit, which was actually meant to serve as a makeshift sling and tourniquet. This was either tied or wrapped around the head, bandanna-style, and often bore legends and slogans. Jim Zwiebel remembered: 'I usually wore a bandanna-type sweatband or nothing at all if we were in "Wait a Minute Vines". The vines would catch on everything, usually pulling off your headgear.' One man in 'Charlie Rangers' wore the same headband for two years, which carried the legend 'It don't mean a thing', thereby advising the enemy that he had no fear of death.

Green and black camouflage face paint made with removable pigment was essential for many Ranger teams on patrol, and resulted in the enemy calling them 'men with painted faces'. According to John L. Rotundo of C Company, mosquito repellent formed a good base and 'helped the cammy stick slide across the face'.

Footwear consisted of Tropical Combat Boots or 'jungle boots', which were introduced to troops in Vietnam along with the combat uniform in 1963. Much of the upper portion of the boot consisted of a green cotton/nylon fabric which was both cool and quick-drying. The lower black leather portion had a sole of a vibram-cleated design, plus two screened eyelets in the instep which afforded drainage and ventilation. The first-pattern boot

Above, Rangers of Team 'Romeo' 15, K Company, 75th Infantry, in distinctive wide-brimmed, Australian bush hats. Team leader Sergeant Luther James Doss stands second from right. All three of his team members (left to right), Charles R. Willard, Jr., Laroy Roth, and Mike Lyne, died on the same mission in January 1970. Refusing non-combat duty, Sergeant Doss bravely returned to active service and paid the ultimate price, being killed in action on 30 April of the same year.
David Doss

Right, this Rip-stop Olive Green Boonie hat was worn by a member of H Company, 1st Air Cavalry, and has been embroidered by a Vietnamese tailor. The division patch on the crown is a Vietnamese-made copy of the cotton twill original. Sewn to the front is a rank patch for a Specialist 4th Class, airborne wings, and combat infantryman badge.

Far right, brown-dominant ERDL Australian bush hat worn by Jim Zwiebel, K Company. Note the embroidered black band, blue beads, and combat infantry badge used to pin up the brim.
Jim Zwiebel

was quickly modified to include reinforced ankles and a steel anti-punji stake insole. Some Rangers ground the tread off their boots in order to leave 'sterile' footprints, while others are believed to have experimented with a variety of allied and enemy footwear, including the rubber tyre-soled Ho Chi Minh sandals. Warren Gallion, 2nd Brigade 'Lurps', 4th Infantry Division, recalled: 'I wore the same boots the whole year I was in Vietnam. They started out as black leather and green canvas. By the end of the year it was impossible to tell the boots had ever been black.'

Regarding underclothing, although the Army issued olive drab T-shirts and boxer shorts, most field soldiers in Vietnam, including LRPs and Rangers, rarely wore underwear except for socks. This prevented jungle rot and rashes, which became rife in the damp, humid jungle climate. When necessary, however, many did wear under their fatigues an olive green nylon/triacetate 'sleep shirt', which kept the chill out when waiting all night in ambush or Night Deployment Perimeter.

WEAPONS

'Everyone had their own way of arming themselves. We were on our own regarding what equipment we took out', recalled Larry Flanagan of K Company. Weaponry carried was dependent on the nature of the assignment. Most men used the standard M16A1 rifle. Designed by Eugene Stoner of the Armalite Division of Fairchild Engine and Airplane Company as the Calibre .223 AR-15, the original M16 was first adopted by the US Air Force. Shortly after this, Colt's Patent Fire Arms Manufacturing Company Inc purchased the manufacturing rights to the weapon, and developed it for the US Army as the M16A1. The principal difference between the M16 and M16A1 was the presence of a bolt-assist plunger mounted on the right rear side of the receiver. This could be used to push the bolt forward if it became stuck due to dirt in the receiver.

The M16A1 was capable of firing its .223 calibre/5.56mm bullets at a rate of 750 to 900 rounds per minute on automatic setting. Alternatively it fired as fast as a man could pull the trigger on semi-automatic. This weapon had an effective range of 435 yards, and its high velocity caused the bullet to tumble on impact, producing a man-stopping wound. It accommodated an M7 Bayonet, and a 'bird cage' flash suppressor. To facilitate night vision, the M16A1 could be fitted with the Starlight scope, a battery-operated night sight worked by magnifying ambient light emitted by stars and moon. Although the small M16 cartridges came in 20-round magazines, usually only 18 rounds were actually loaded to reduce spring pressure and resultant jamming. A spare magazine was sometimes taped to the one in the rifle for rapid reloading. Thirty-round magazines became available later in the war, and saw some use with the Rangers. 'A lot of us had noise suppressors on our weapons', recalled Daniel Pope of C Company. 'These were in the early stages of development and there were a lot of them put into the field for testing. Mine was given to me by Mitch Werbel of Sionics Inc, and it proved to be the most effective advantage I had in a fire fight.'

Depending on availability, many Rangers preferred to pack the Colt Automatic Rifle, or CAR-15, which was the sub-machine gun version of the M16. Officially known as the XM-177E1, it was chambered for the calibre .223, or 5.56 mm cartridge, and normally used a 20-round magazine. The original Model E-1 had a 10-inch barrel, and was 28.7 inches long overall. It weighed 5.9 pounds loaded, and had a telescoping buttstock. The later Model E-2 had an 11.5 inch long barrel. The increased noise and fireball produced by this short-barrelled CAR-15 proved to be a major operational limitation, but was overcome to a certain extent by the addition of a flash suppressor. Bearing on its receiver the manufacturer's stamp -'COLT COMMANDO',

Right from top to bottom, Ron Coon, 2nd Brigade LRP, 4th Infantry Division, is pictured here holding an M 79 40mm grenade launcher or 'thump gun', with CAR-15 slung over his shoulder. On this particular reconnaissance mission on the Cambodian border, he wore a North Vietnamese uniform. He recalled: 'I only wore that uniform twice. The second time I saw the error of my ways. We were coming out of a hot LZ. When I broke out of the bush, the door gunner just about nailed me.' *Ron Coon*

Bob Crawford, 4th Infantry Division LRRPs, armed with the CAR 15 or XM 177E1. Bob recollected: 'I always carried a CAR 15 with no less than 25 magazines, the first magazine was loaded with nine tracers and nine regular shells, every other one was a tracer. The other mags were loaded so every fifth round was a tracer.' Note the 'fish-pole' antenna of his PRC 25 radio tucked over his left shoulder. *Ron Coon*

Sergeant Ted Yoshimura, H Company (Ranger), 75th Infantry, armed with an AK 47 and wearing North Vietnamese Army web gear. According to Sergeant Yoshimura: 'I remember that soon after volunteering for the LRRPs, I was told by one of the men that I could fool the enemy by using and wearing NVA equipment.' *Ted Yoshimura*

Glen McCrary, H Company, 75th Infantry (Airborne), with M203 combination of M16 rifle and 40mm pump-action grenade launcher tube. He also wears a Grenade Carrier Vest, which was more widely issued in Vietnam by 1970. Ranger Clarence Monroe offers encouragement behind him. *Glen McCrary*

the CAR-15 was a reminder to Vietnam War Rangers that the weapon most sought after by the Texas Rangers during the war with Mexico, 123 years earlier, was also produced by the Colt Company.

Patrols given recondo-style missions often included a sniper usually armed with a 7.62mm M14 rifle complete with scope sight. Originally intended to replace the Browning Automatic Rifle as a squad automatic weapon, the M14 was capable of automatic as well as semi-automatic fire. In the right hands it had an accurate range of over 300 yards.

Captured enemy weapons were also very popular with LRPs and Rangers. Known as the 'peasant rifle', the AK-47 was prized for its dependability and stopping power. Larry Flanagan, K Company, recollected: 'Some of the Rangers took out AK 47s, a couple had British Sten guns with silencers. We also had M14s, Swedish Ks, and M60 machine guns if we wanted them, but I only remember the machine guns being used just once.' Adopted for service with the Soviet Army in 1949, the Kalashnikov 7.62 x 39mm calibre, selective fire assault rifle was the main infantry weapon of the NVA and Viet Cong. It carried a 30-round magazine and had a killing range of 1,500 metres. Also favoured was the SKS45 carbine, and the RPD, nicknamed the 'Rapid People Destroyer'. Developed by Ruchnol Pulemet Degtyarev, it was adopted as the standard squad automatic weapon of the Soviet Army in 1948. All three weapons were chambered for the Model 43 intermediate cartridge.

The Swedish K40 was supplied to the LRPs and, subsequently, to the Rangers by the Army Special Forces. Tom Reed of 2nd Brigade LRPs, 4th Infantry Division, and later Company Armorer of K Company, 75th Infantry, recalled: 'My weapon of choice was the Swedish K, a sub-machine gun that held a 35-round magazine and fired a healthy 9-mm pistol round. The fact that it fired 200 rounds

Above left, the .223 calibre/5.56mm M16A1 rifle was carried by many Rangers during the Vietnam War. *Author/Alex Allen and Neil Holdom*

Above right, the sub-machine gun version of the M 16, the Colt 5.56mm CAR 15, or XM 177E1. *Author/Alex Allen and Neil Holdom*

Right, lime-green dominant ERDL poncho and liner. In the steaming heat of the jungles and forests of South Vietnam, the liner was generally used on its own, protecting LRPs and Rangers from both the intense heat and the torrential rainfall. *Author/Alex Allen and Neil Holdom*

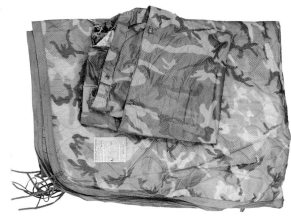

a minute slower than the M-16 was to me an advantage, because it meant that the bad guys would have to keep their heads down that much longer. I carried 11 magazines for the K and an extra 100 round box in my pack.'

According to Don Ericson of 'Charlie Rangers', 75th Infantry: 'The American [M3] grease gun could stop an elephant in its tracks at close range but was basically useless at any distance. The .45 calibre Thompson machine gun was also at our disposal but had the same characteristics of the grease gun, and was very heavy. We also had some 12-gauge, pump shotguns floating around the company, but they were rarely used because of the dense vegetation in our usual AOs [Area of Operations]. A few twelve-gauge shotguns were cut down (stocks and barrels), and used as secondary weapons; their short length, about two feet, made them easy to fasten to the back of the ruck-sack. In a close contact, the killing pattern of a sawed-off shotgun would have been awesome. We had heard that the modifications were against the Geneva Convention but I don't think that anyone cared.'

Staff Sergeant Gene Boyd of the 'Riverine Rangers' recollected: 'I had a cut-down version of the M-2 Carbine... a cute little rig, cut off at the handle grip and sawed off at the nose. I used it to direct fire, with red tracers, in hard times when a position had already been given up.'

On occasion, some Ranger teams were armed entirely with captured weapons, especially if they were donning enemy uniforms. Generally speaking, new men had to earn the right to carry a communist-made weapon, if possible by taking one from an enemy soldier in combat. A major advantage in packing these sidearms was that they sounded different from an M16 or CAR-15, hence their use did not automatically alert the enemy. A disadvantage was that, on most occasions, you heard the enemy rather than saw him, and this sometimes resulted in teams receiving friendly fire.

Pistols or revolvers were a valuable part of the Rangers' arsenal. Most commonly used was the Colt M1911A1 .45 calibre semi-automatic pistol which had given faithful service to the US military since before the First World War. Bob Crawford, 4th Infantry Division LRRPs, remembered: 'I carried a match grade 45 automatic that I smuggled into Vietnam with me. I only ever fired it at the range, it was just my security blanket.' Jim Zwiebel, of K Company, recalled: 'We had another man called "Ratman" Thibodeau that carried a .357 in a shoulder holster to take in tunnels with him.'

Another popular handgun was the Browning Hi-Power 9-mm, which held a larger 13-round magazine. The 9mm Smith and Wesson MK.22 Model O with silencer was known as the 'Hush Puppy', due to its original use to kill enemy sentry dogs. Hence all firearms fitted with silencers were eventually called 'Hush Puppies'. The single-shot Hi-Standard .22 calibre pistol, originally used by the OSS during the Second World War, was available for special missions. With a silencer attached, and loaded with a hollow round, the .22 could quietly take out a lone enemy sentry when required.

Rangers also had access to the full range of heavier weapons available in Vietnam, such as M67 90mm Recoilless Rifles, M79 and XM-148 grenade launchers, and rocket-firing M72 Light Anti-Tank Weapons (LAWs). The LAW was a fibreglass, collapsible rocket launcher which was fired once then thrown away. Normally used in Vietnam for 'bunker busting', it delivered an effective counter-punch and tended to demoralise the North Vietnamese troops. Mopping up after fire fights, the Rangers sometimes discovered that the enemy had abandoned dead comrades and valuable equipment to get away from LAW rocket blasts.

Toward the end of the war, many teams started carrying the 7.62mm M60 Machine Gun for extra fire power. Never issued, they were

Below far left, **An olive drab nylon and mesh Grenade Carrier Vest which closed with Velcro strips and a row of press-studs. This carried a maximum of 24 rounds in three rows of pockets on each side of the front. The lower two rows were designed to contain high explosive and multiple projectile rounds, while the top row held the longer parachute signal rounds.** *Below left*, **the mesh back could be adjusted by a buckled strap.** *Author/Alex Allen and Neil Holdom*

Below, reconstruction of a member of E Company 'Go Devils' operating out of Dong Tam. He wears a lime-dominant ERDL uniform and in-country-made Boonie hat with field dressing pocket on the crown.
Below left, across his chest he carries extra M16A1 magazines in a seven-pocket bandolier. Over his left shoulder is an M18A1 Anti-Personnel Mine Carrier, commonly called a 'Claymore bag'. Secured to the right side of his H-Harness is a strobe light in its nylon pouch, underneath which is a pink right-angle flashlight, normally used by 'tunnel rats'. A M1956 First Aid/Compass Pouch is fastened to the left shoulder strap, beneath which is slung a rope on a snap link, used for making a Swiss seat for rappelling. Attached to his M1956 belt, with Davis Quick-release buckle, are two M1956 universal small arms ammo pouches, plus several smoke grenades and a 'baseball' fragmentation grenade. He holds the standard M16A1 rifle with an AN/PVS-2B Starlight Scope, a battery-run night sight operated by magnifying the ambient light emitted by the stars and the moon. Note his Lowland ERDL camouflage trousers are tied just below the knee to prevent bugs from crawling up his legs.
Below right, he carries the much-preferred Tropical Rucksack, on top of which is strapped the standard heavyweight olive poncho. Two parachute flares can be seen sticking out of the middle pocket. A pair of M1950 leather gloves are attached by a snaplink to the straps of the rucksack. These were used when the Ranger had to rappel from the helicopter to the ground when being inserted by helicopter over dense jungle. Secured to the rear of his belt is a two-quart canteen in its nylon carrier, and a nylon 20-round magazine pouch.
Author/Alex Allen and Neil Holdom

often acquired from downed helicopters. Although it weighed 23.75 lbs and had a fierce kick, the firepower of the M60 often gave the Ranger the edge when drawn into fire fights. Team 3-3, 'Charlie Rangers', called their M60 'The Gun'. On their last mission out of Pleiku in April 1970, John Rotundo carried it: 'I chambered a 25-round teaser belt, all tracers for effect, and 600 rounds, while each member also carried 100 rounds, giving us a little over 1,100 rounds of M 60 ammo.... The weight of the gun, which was supported by a rope tied to the barrel on the front end and around the stock on the rear, would let it hang from my neck when breaking the bush. As clumsy as the rig sounds, it didn't affect our noise on that mission.'

Many LRP and Ranger teams began to carry at least one 'thump gun', properly called the M-79 40mm grenade launcher. Also in use by 1970 was the M203 combination of M16 rifle with a 40mm pump-action grenade launcher tube slung underneath. This enabled the grenadier to continue using his rifle in a fire fight after his grenade rounds had been expended.

A range of grenades were also carried in either bandoliers or bags. White phosphorus, or 'Willie Peter', grenades were used for their blast-and-burn impact. Burning phosphorus struck terror in the

heart of the enemy as it could not be smothered or removed, and burned through flesh and bone. The smokescreen it threw up also obscured the Ranger from his prey. M26 fragmentation grenades were used for killing, while concussion grenades stunned the enemy, and were particularly useful for taking prisoners. Ron Coon, 2nd Brigade 'Lurps', 4th Infantry Division, recalled: 'I always carried one fragmentation grenade in my pants pocket. I always figured if I lost everything, and I did crossing a river once, then at least I would have something.' Some Ranger grenadiers cut down the M 79 to pistol-size and used one quart canteen covers as holsters. Frank Benns of 'Charlie Rangers' carried a sawn-off M 79 tucked inside his rucksack so that he could reach over his right shoulder and snap it into action when needed.

M18 smoke grenades were used to mark pick-up zones or to identify targets for tactical air support and gunships. Various colours were employed, as the enemy often created their own smokescreen in an attempt to confuse Ranger air support. The Ranger ground team would pop a smoke grenade colour of their choice to mark their position, and wait for the helicopter pilot to check which colour they were using. Once this had been confirmed, an extraction could take place. Teams also spread out bright orange and purple plastic

panels, or used a signal mirror flash, or strobe light, to indicate their location.

Although knives were carried by Rangers, they were used mainly for hacking through the jungle rather than for combat. Often carried with handle facing down in a scabbard taped to the left shoulder of the 'H-harness', popular blades included the 'Aircrew Survival Knife' and the 'K-Bar' utility/fighting knife. Emmett Mulroney, Team 'Hawkeye 1 Alpha', K Company, claimed: 'I carried a hatchet and sometimes a machete'.

Gas, mines, and explosives were as important to the Ranger as his rifle and rations. CS tear gas was employed to enable a team to break contact with the enemy. When pulling out of a fire fight, Rangers would attempt to head upwind, opening their gas canisters as they withdrew. According to Don Ericson of 'Charlie Rangers': 'The claymore [mine] was a perfect tool for a Ranger ambush.' Consisting of a convex, rectangular plastic case measuring 8.5 by 3.2 inches, the M 18A1 Claymore (from Gaelic *'claidheamh mor'*) anti-personnel mine was indeed an essential part of the Ranger's arsenal. Inside the front of the case was over 700 steel balls embedded in plastic, behind which was 24 ounces of C-4 plastic explosive charge. Transported in its own carry-case, the mine was normally command-detonated using the M57 firing device which consisted of 100 feet of wire, an M4 blasting cap, and a charging handle or 'klacker'. They could also be triggered via a tripwire or booby trap. When the charge was detonated, the steel balls sprayed out a 60-degree fragmentation pattern to a maximum lethal distance of 50 metres and a height of about two metres. The mines could be used individually or 'daisy-chained' together with a detonator cord and fired in multiples. They could also be placed so that the back blast rather than 'buckshot' struck the enemy, making it possible for prisoners to be taken.

Another weapon employed to great effect by Rangers was the M14, nicknamed the 'shoe', or 'toe popper', mine. Designed to maim not kill, this

A tear gas, or CN DM, canister and an M14 Incendiary Grenade are attached to the loops on the CIDG Rucksack in this reconstruction. Tear gas made the enemy's eyes water and skin burn. Thermite-filled incendiary grenades were used to destroy caches of enemy food and equipment. Of interest is an early cotton duck two-quart canteen slung on the back of the ruck.
Author/Alex Allen and Neil Holdom

tiny mine weighed only 3.3 ounces and measured 2.2 inches in diameter by 1.7 inches in height. It was mainly used to cover avenues of approach to an ambush or a defensive position that could not be protected by direct fire. An added advantage of the 'shoe mine' was that it was triggered by pressure and did not need the Ranger who placed it to remain in the area. Its blast was lethal up to one metre, and caused terrible casualties up to 25 metres. Furthermore, the mine's explosion was not unlike mortar or artillery fire, which confused the enemy as to whether or not opposing soldiers were nearby.

Tear gas, or CN-DM, canisters were carried attached to loops on the ruck or web gear. This made the enemy's eyes water, skin burn, and caused general discomfort. CS gas canisters were also carried, and were much more effective, burning nose, eyes, throat, and lungs, as well as skin. Breathing was also greatly inhibited, and the victim tended to vomit.

EQUIPMENT

A wide variety of US, enemy, and home-made web equipment was used to sustain a Ranger on an average four-day mission in the jungles of Vietnam. Bob Crawford of 4th Infantry Division LRRPs recalled: 'I had a set of web gear that was World War Two or Korean War era. It had six built-in pockets that held four magazines each. I added two canteen pouches that held hand grenades each. I wore my .45 in a shoulder holster under my left arm. I carried two extra clips for it. I had my survival knife taped to the left suspender of my web gear.'

Standard gear for many Rangers still consisted of the M1956 Load Bearing Equipment (LBE) Individual Equipment Belt of olive green cotton-canvas with blackened alloy fittings. First introduced in 1957 to accommodate the M14 rifle, a wide range of ammunition pouches, canteens, grenades, and other equipment could be attached to the belt via a new vertical slide-keeper system.

The more modern M1967 nylon pistol belt was later fitted with the Davis quick release buckle, which enabled the wearer to open the belt with only one hand. Sometimes the belt opened on its own. The belt was supported by the M1956 Belt Suspenders, or H-harness, which was lightly padded in order to distribute the weight more evenly over the shoulders.

Most commonly worn on the belt was the M1956 Universal Small Arms Ammunition Pouch. As this model was originally designed to take the larger 7.62mm M14 magazines, some men padded the bottom of the pouch in order to raise up the shorter M16 magazines. Also available to a lesser degree was the purpose-made 'Small Arms Ammunition Pouch M16A1', and the M1967 nylon pouches which were after the same pattern. All models carried a maximum of four 20-round magazines, and were given additional support via a strap secured to the suspenders. It was common for LRPs and Rangers to utilize M1956/67 canteen covers in lieu of pouches to carry rifle magazines or grenades, due to their larger capacity.

Extra rifle ammunition was commonly carried slung across the chest, or belt-style around the waist, in a cotton bandolier capable of holding seven 20-round magazines apiece. Also popular was the old M1937 Browning Automatic Rifle (BAR) Belt. Originally designed to take two BAR magazines in each of its six pockets, the BAR belt could carry twice that number of M16 magazines, and/or a number of grenades. Some men wore captured vest-type Communist-manufactured AK 47 chest harnesses, the pouches of which held the later-pattern 30-round magazine. Yet more magazines might also be carried in the rucksack. Emmett Mulroney, K Company, recalled: 'I carried out two bandoliers of loaded M16 magazines across my chest, another 10 magazines in my pockets and five to 10 more in my back pack, along with several boxes of M16 rounds – if the M79 was taken on a mission, we each carried four

Opposite, **Private First Class, Charlie Rangers, 75th Infantry (Airborne), 1970,** wearing a Tigerstripe camouflaged uniform produced in Vietnam. Typically, his Boonie hat has grenade ring pulls tucked into the foliage loops. His face is daubed with Army camouflage paint, while around his neck is an olive drab bandage or 'drive-on rag'. His Recon gloves consist of the M1950 Leather Glove – Strap Closure with the fingers and thumbs partially cut off, permitting unimpeded use of weapons

and gear while protecting the hands from vines and thorns. On his feet are second-pattern Tropical Combat Boots with reinforced ankles and anti-punji-spike soles. A dog tag was often laced into one of the boots to aid the process of identification in case of the loss of the tags worn around the neck.

The Ranger holds a M 203 rifle/launcher combination. An Aircrew Survival Knife is taped handle down to the left shoulder on his STABO harness, while attached to the right shoulder is a canvas

first aid/compass pouch. In a rear view detail (top right) he carries a light weight canvas indigenous ruck with three cargo pockets. Modelled on a captured NVA pattern, and originally issued to members of the Civilian Irregular Defence Group, it would have been procured through the Special Forces and made in Okinawa. He is surrounded by weapons and equipment: (top) a Colt 5.56mm CAR-15 carbine and 20-round magazine (note the cleaning rod from a standard M16 rifle taped along the

front and rear sights.
Carried in this fashion, the rod could be quickly employed to remove an unextracted round during a fire fight); (middle right) load bearing equipment, consisting of a M1967 nylon pistol belt fitted with the Davis quick release buckle, attached to which is a M1956 Universal Small Arms Ammunition Pouch and a M1967 nylon canteen cover, both of which contain 20-round magazines of M16 ammunition; (bottom right) Aircrew Survival Knife,

sheath, and sharpener; nylon five-quart canteen; later model two-quart canteen; (bottom) machete and sheath; (top left) M18A1 Claymore anti-personnel mine containing approximately 700 steel balls embedded in plastic; (middle left) XM28 Lightweight Protective Mask; first-pattern Tropical Combat Boots; (bottom left) M67 'baseball' Grenade; M18 Coloured Smoke Grenades; M26A1 Fragmentation Grenade.
Painting by Richard Hook.

Below, the radio-telephone operator (RTO) in this reconstruction would have been on a short patrol, and carries a AN/PRC-77 short-range FM radio on its cotton-duck carrying frame. He holds the standard H-189 handset. Note the taped antenna. The spare parts bag seen on the left side of the radio carried a spare battery, handset, and sectional antenna. Attached to the back of the radio is an Airpanel Marker, a CS gas grenade, and several coloured smoke grenades. *Below right*, detail showing top of AN/PRC-77 radio. *Author/Alex Allen and Neil Holdom*

explosive and one CS Gas round.'

A maximum of six grenade rounds could be carried in a purpose-made bandolier worn either across the chest or around the waist. From 1968 onwards, a nylon and mesh Grenade Carrier Vest was in use which closed with Velcro strips and a row of press-studs, and carried a maximum of 24 rounds in three rows of pockets on each side of the front. The lower two rows were designed to contain high explosive and multiple projectile rounds, while the top row held the longer parachute signal rounds. The mesh back could be adjusted by a buckled strap.

Water was essential in the steamy jungles and forests of Vietnam. By 1969, the stainless steel/aluminium M1910-type canteen, with World War Two era black plastic ribbed twist-cap, had largely been superseded by an olive drab one-quart plastic model which was first standardized in 1962. This was carried in the M1956 felt-lined web cover until the introduction of the M1967 lightweight nylon cover. A semi-rigid two-quart rubberized canteen was also popular. It was quieter to carry and flexible enough to be rolled and stored in the rucksack when empty. The canteen itself was made of ethylene acetate with a black twist-cap. The second pattern two-quart cover was first produced unlined and made of heavy, grey-green, water-proof cotton-canvas. Later pattern covers were produced in a nylon duck, lined with a synthetic pile intended to keep the water cool. Both types of covers had slide-keepers for attachment to web gear or rucksack harness, plus removable carrying-straps, plastic fasteners, and a small pocket for water purification tablets.

The Five Quart Flotation Bladder was introduced in 1968 and consisted of a collapsible, clear vinyl bladder carried in a olive drab nylon cover with tie-down cords at each corner. Water was dispensed via a canteen-like cap with a removeable filter. The instructions printed on the front explain how to fill it from a stream.

The reverse side has details explaining how to remove the clear bladder from the nylon carrier. When empty, this canteen was very easily rolled up and stored inside the rucksack. These canteens were unpopular with Rangers because of their fragile construction. Also attached either to the suspenders or belt was a M1956 first aid/compass pouch containing field dressing or lensatic compass.

To accommodate heavier gear, the LRP and Ranger carried rucksacks of various manufacture. In general use was the lightweight rucksack, which was developed in 1962 and was becoming more widely available by 1965. This weighed only three pounds when empty and consisted of a water resistant nylon bag, with three external pockets, attached to a tubular aluminium frame. As originally supplied, the bag was fixed to the bottom of the frame, although it could be field-modified to hang from the top. The adjustable strap clips which closed the ruck were usually taped-up to prevent them rattling against the frame, and numerous pieces of equipment could be attached to the hangers on the sides of the bag or to the straps on the frame.

Sergeant Ronald Christopher, LRRP detachment, 1st Cavalry Division, experimented with the Australian Ruck Sack (lightweight) without a frame in January 1967, and recalled: 'The rucksack rode down on the hips and nothing we could do would keep it up on the shoulders. It might have had something to do with the weight we carried, but I think the rucksack may have had a design flaw. A supply sergeant, Mike Hammer, acquired some back pack frames and that cured the problem! The frame also helped my ATL carry the radio. The metal frame had one problem, but we took care of that with tape, to keep the sun from reflecting off the metal.' According to Warren Gallion, who volunteered for LRP service from a mechanized infantry unit in the 4th Infantry Division in 1968: 'When I joined the LRPs it

was my first experience with a metal frame pack. I was taught how to tie the radio in next to my shoulders to distribute the weight. The multiple pockets made it easy to store and get to different items in an emergency.'

Also popular with the Rangers was the 'indigenous ruck' procured through the Special Forces and made in Okinawa. Modelled on a captured North Vietnamese Army pattern, and originally issued to members of the Civilian Irregular Defence Group (CIDG), these rucksacks had three cargo pockets fitted on the sides and back, and were very simply constructed from a stiff waterproof-treated grey-green canvas, although a few were made of untreated olive drab canvas.

The ARVN rucksack, first produced for the South Vietnamese Rangers, was also used by American LRPs and Rangers. Another lightweight rucksack of cotton-duck, with two large external pockets, it was fastened on a sprung metal

Strobe lights were used to signal to aircraft overhead. Seen here is the SDU/5E Strobe Light with flash shield, which enabled the light to be seen from the air only.
Author/Alex Allen and Neil Holdom

A unit-one medic bag with three-zipped compartments containing medical supplies including morphine, field dressings, tourniquets, and a surgical kit consisting of scalpels, clamps and scissors. The bag was made of cotton duck and had a single shoulder strap. All team members were trained in advanced First Aid at the Recondo School in Nha Trang. Although all members were trained, only one man would carry the team medic bag.
Author/Alex Allen and Neil Holdom

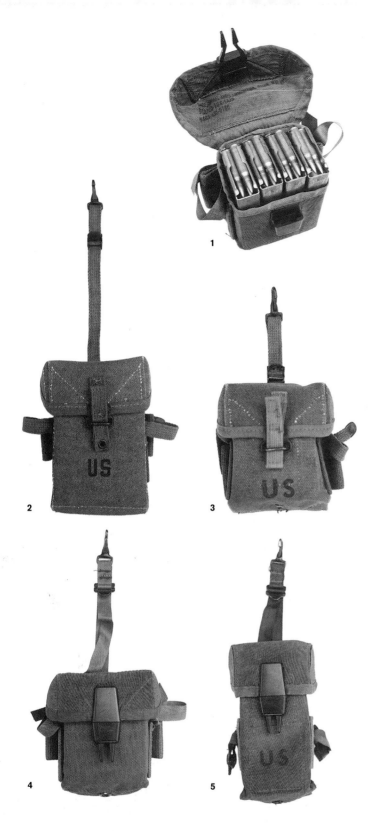

X-frame which held the bag away from the back, and permitted ready access to the rear of the pistol belt. Prototypes of a new and larger nylon rucksack were sent to Vietnam in late 1965. After some alterations, the Tropical Ruck was standardized on 4 March 1968. This had one large main bag and three smaller pockets, each being secured with two plastic snaps. Weighing less empty than the lightweight ruck, it had a similar frame to the ARVN Ranger model, and was the largest US carrying system available.

Whichever type was used, the rucksack usually weighed between 70 and 80 pounds when packed for a short-range patrol or mission – it was much heavier on longer operations. As Rick Ehrler, E Company, 50th Infantry (LRP), who operated in the Mekong Delta, recalled: 'When the mud got thick, I was walking deep!' The Ranger developed various ways of hauling himself up once the rucksack was on his back. Ron Edwards, L Company (Ranger), 75th Infantry, remembered: 'I usually had to sit down with my back to it, slide my arms through the straps, roll over on my hands and knees, then use my weapon to brace me while I stood up. No, we did not move fast or far quickly, but we did move carefully!'

RATIONS

By 1969, the heavy tinned C-rations had largely given way to dehydrated rations packed in plastic bags. Originally produced for Special Forces and reconnaissance personnel, they were readily available to Rangers. Becoming known as 'Lurp' rations, they were much sought after by all units before the end of the war. Initially most savoury meals tasted the same, but this was improved after rations were freeze-dried rather than dehydrated. 'Lurp' meals included beef stew, chicken with rice, spaghetti with meat sauce, and chili with beans. According to Emmett Mulroney, K Company, carried four to six LRRP rations' per man on their missions in the Central Highlands. Tom Reed,

Above left
(1) the US ammunition pouch accommodated a maximum of four 20-round magazines for the M16 rifle or CAR15. These were often supplemented by carrying more magazines in M1956/67 canteen covers, which had a larger capacity. **(2) M1956 Universal Small Arms Ammunition Pouch.** Designed to take the larger 7.62mm M14 magazines, these were often padded out at the bottom to raise up the shorter M16 magazines. **(3) Purpose-made Small Arms Ammunition Pouch M16A1.** **(4) M1967 experimental 30-round magazine pouch** for the M16A1 rifle. **(5) M1967 nylon M14 pouch.** *Author/Alex Allen and Neil Holdom*

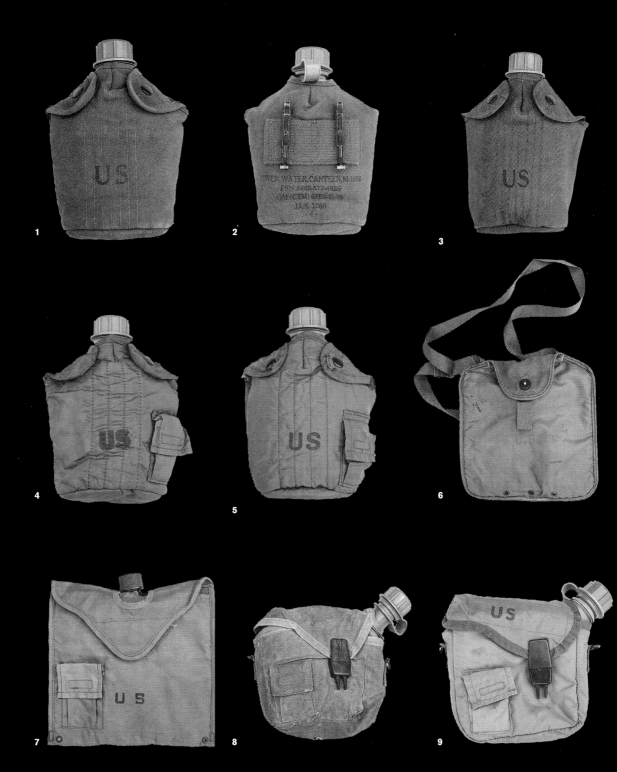

Above

LRPS and Rangers carried as many one-quart canteens as was practicable, and attached them to their belts via vertical slide-keepers. The covers were also used for extra ammunition and grenades.

(1 & 2) M1956 web cover, and reverse showing slide-keepers.

3) Improved web cover with nylon edging.

(4) First pattern M1967 nylon cover with plastic snaps, which came into service in 1968.

(5) Second pattern 1967 cover with metal snaps, circa 1969-74. Note the water purification pocket added to the nylon covers.

(6) Experimental two-quart nylon canteen and cover, very similar to the canvas World War Two jungle canteen. Dated 1963, this item had a non-removable carrying strap, but was originally designed to fit inside the main compartment flap of the lightweight rucksack.

(7) Commonly referred to as the first pattern two-quart canteen, and in use between 1965-67, this model had metal slide keepers for attaching to the web belt or rucksack. Note the water purification tablet pocket.

(8) An early cotton duck two-quart canteen. These covers were unlined and had slide keepers for attachment to a belt or rucksack. This model also had a detachable carrying strap.

(9) Last model two-quart canteen made for Vietnam service. The cover was nylon with a pile lining. This item is dated 1969, although they were produced from 1968 through 1974.

Author/Alex Allen and N eil Holdom

2nd Brigade LRPs, 4th Infantry Division, recollected: 'When we started I liked them all – by the time I left the only one I could stand was the Chili. I ate cold rations in the field and the chili beans never quite lost their crunch. It was sort of like having chili with crackers that never got soggy. I ate cold rations for two reasons. First, the smell of hot rations travelled much farther than cold, and second, to cook the rations you needed a canteen cup, which was an extra piece of metal to clank against things and make noise.' 'Lurp' rations were supplemented by a vanilla, chocolate, or coconut candy wafer which the troops usually referred to as John Wayne bars.

Only rarely did Rangers have the opportunity to heat food by using a heat tab, which looked like a small bar of blue soap. These were slow to heat and emitted a noxious odour likely to gas the cook and alert the enemy to the Rangers' position. A better field expedient for heating water was C4. A small piece of plastic explosive, this burned intensely and could bring water to the boil in under a minute. This could then be poured into the freeze-dried food and allowed to set for about five to 10 minutes, after which it was ready to eat. Nonetheless, the cook had to be careful not to smother the flame once lit, as it would explode. Care was also needed not to get C4 crumbs in the food or water as it was very harmful to the nervous system.

Medical supplies were essential to LRPs and Rangers, not only to treat wounds but also to combat the multitude of infections and diseases found in the jungle. Teams varied regarding the means they employed to carry medical equipment. In most cases, an assistant team leader (ATL) or another patrol member was responsible for a large team aid bag, while each man carried a small first-aid packet. Such supplies were only ever intended for short term treatment in order to stabilize the casualty until he could be lifted out by helicopter. Drugs carried included anti-malaria tablets, such as chloroquine primaquine, a large orange tablet taken once a week, and dapsone, a small white pill required once a day. Other drugs consisted of 'uppers' such as dextroamphetamine, or 'greenies', which assisted the Ranger in keeping awake on extended missions.

Individual first-aid packets included a bandage compress complete with attached gauze wrapping, which protected the wound and helped to control bleeding. A vital medical aid was Serum Albumin, a blood volume expander used to maintain the blood pressure of a severely wounded man until he could be evacuated. Often carried taped to the suspender yoke behind the neck, it came in a grey metal container about the size of a small beer can,

and was injected into the vein of the casualty via a large syringe. Morphine came packed in quarter-grain syrettes with a needle that could be fixed on the nipple end. The drug could be speedily administered by rolling the syrette up like a toothpaste tube. Rangers frequently carried their own supply of morphine. Some men wore a syrette in a protective holder around their necks, along with their dog tags, and stories abound of men being wounded, administering their own morphine, bandaging themselves up, and rejoining the action.

In order to report what they observed and heard, and to call in support when required, the Rangers carried a number of communication systems. Most commonly used was the partially transistorised AN/PRC25 short-range FM radio or the fully transistorized and slightly more reliable PRC77, which looked virtually identical. Unlovingly called the 'Prick-25' by the troops, the former weighed over 24 pounds with a battery, which had an average operating life of a little over 20 hours. It was issued with a cotton-duck carrying pack, but the radio was usually carried inside the rucksack with antenna and handset outside. The enemy would target the radioman first to prevent extraction of the team or artillery strikes being called in. If it was not so obvious who had the radio, it made a less identifiable target.

Each radio set was issued with a short tape antenna and a longer, seven-section 'fish-pole' antenna which could be packed away. Terrain permitting, the average optimum range of these radios was only about 3.5 miles. A range of field-expedient antennas, often made from WD-1 communication wire, could extend this up to as much as seven miles. The headset could be used in conjunction with an integral boom-type microphone, or either an H-189 or H-138 handset. If the latter became wet, the entire system tended to short out, but this could be partially overcome by simply wrapping the handset in a plastic bag that was issued with the battery.

Tom Reed, 2nd Brigade 'Lurps', 4th Infantry Division, recalled: 'I'm thoroughly convinced that the Army kept all the new radios back in the States where they would look good on inspection and sent all the cruddy ones to Vietnam. The problems were so numerous that after a while they started sending two radios out with each team to make sure they would have one that worked. The battery life was extremely short. You felt incredibly lucky if you got a long antennae that was still strung together. Usually they were in pieces and had to be put together like a puzzle.' According to Warren Gallion, of the same unit: 'The major complaint I recall about the PRC25 was the weight. Like most radios it was line of sight, so it was easy to get out of radio range in the Highlands. I was extended on one mission and I was down to my last battery before being extracted. As much as we complained about it, I can't imagine us doing the job without the "Prick-25"!'

The URC-68, a longer range, but heavier, radio was occasionally used by Rangers engaged in missions at greater distances from friendly support. Also carried at the team leader's discretion was a small survival radio, normally used by air force and army aviators. These varied from pure transmitters used to bring in extraction helicopters, to short-range, hand-size receiver/transmitter sets, such as the URC-10 and URC-64, that permitted personnel to contact aircraft overhead.

Other special equipment made available to Rangers on a mission-requirement basis included rappel ropes, rope ladders and the STABO extraction harness. The former consisted of two 120-foot-long nylon rope and tackle systems used for insertion to, and extraction from, the landing zone via helicopter. The rope cargo ladder was 30 feet in length with the middle portion normally secured to floor rings on the helicopter's cargo hold. When released, the ladder was lowered simultaneously from both sides of the aircraft for the men to either descend or ascend. In an area with high vegetation, only one end of the ladder would be dropped to a maximum length of 28 feet.

The STABO harness, named in honour of its three recondo-school instructor/inventors, Major Robert L. Stevens, Captain John D. H. Knabb, and Sergeant First Class Clifford L. Roberts, was used when operating in areas of thick jungle, or difficult terrain, or in known enemy strongholds, when an extraction on the move was the only way to survive. The STABO was worn as the suspender on the LBE, with the bottom straps rolled up while on patrol and only connected between the legs to the front part of the harness prior to extraction. Two ropes with snap links at the end were dropped from the hovering

chopper, and were snap-linked on to the rings on the shoulders of the harness. This kept the soldier's hands free to operate his weapon at all times during extraction. Once securely fastened, he was lifted out and remained suspended underneath the craft until a convenient landing site became available to lower him back to the ground.

The McGuire rig was named in honour of Project Delta Sergeant Major Charles T. McGuire, and was in service before the introduction of the STABO harness. To use this system, the 'Lurp' carried tightly coiled, six-foot sling ropes connected to their web gear with a snap link. These ropes were used to tie 'Swiss seats' around the man's hips and thighs, following which they were secured to the rappel rope or the rig via a snap link. The sling rope also served to tie up prisoners, or as a safety line when crossing a stream. Alternatively they could be tugged on, as a signalling device during darkness, if the rope was run from man to man.

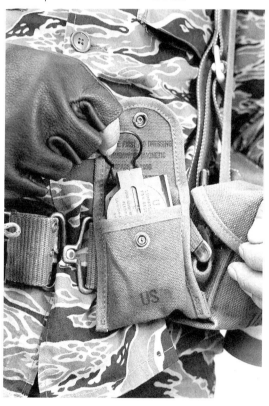

A lensatic compass being drawn from the First Aid/Compass pouch attached to this M1956 individual equipment belt.

The compass being used in conjunction with a map. *Author/Alex Allen and Neil Holdom*

RANGER LEGACY

With the withdrawal of US troops from the war in Vietnam in 1973, only Ranger companies A and B were retained in service. The outbreak of the Yom Kippur War in the Middle East during the same year prompted the US Department of the Army to consider the need for a light mobile force capable of being quickly deployed to any trouble spot in the world. The following year, Army Chief of Staff General Creighton Abrams called for the establishment of a permanent Ranger presence in the US Army and the 1st and 2nd Battalions, 75th Infantry (Ranger), were formed, using the men of the surviving two companies as a cadre.

While missions in Vietnam had mainly involved raids, ambushes, and reconnaissance, the changing face of war required the modern Ranger to meet the challenge of more direct-action missions and less reconnaissance work. In fact, the US Army created other LRRP units to focus on reconnaissance and intelligence gathering. The Rangers went on to participate in numerous international crises and wars during the remainder of the 20th century, and made their mark as one of the world's premier direct-fire combat assault forces.

During April 1980, the Rangers were involved as a support force in the ill-fated 'Desert One' attempt to rescue more than 50 Americans held hostage by Iran in the American embassy in Teheran. Although primarily a Special Forces operation, C Company, 1st Ranger Battalion, was assigned the task of securing a landing area for MC-130 transport planes at Manazariyeh, 35 miles south of Teheran. Known by the Rangers as 'Operation Eagle Claw', they were to land if possible, or jump if necessary, and once the airfield had been seized, hold it while C 141 jet Starlifters arrived to take the hostages and their Special Forces rescuers to Egypt. Unfortunately 'Desert One' was aborted at the first stage when the mission suffered excessive problems and lost too many helicopters to continue the mission. After issue of the abort order, one of the

RH 53D choppers crashed into a Lockheed C130 Hercules creating a huge fireball. Five US Air Force crewmen and three Marines perished. A second mission was never attempted and the hostages were finally released in January 1981.

The Rangers had little time to prepare for their role in Operation 'Urgent Fury', the US invasion of Grenada on 25 October 1983, following the *coup d'état* which overthrew the democratic government of Prime Minister Eric M. Gairy. The 1st and 2nd Battalions led the way with a daring low-level parachute assault, following which they seized the airfield at Point Salines, with a loss of five Rangers dead and six wounded. During several aborted attempts to rescue political prisoners and American students from nearby complexes, several Rangers were badly hurt while air-assaulting in UH 60 Black Hawk helicopters. A full-scale helicopter swoop on Calivigny Barracks on 27 October resulted in three of four troop-carrying Black Hawks being downed as they smashed into one another on landing. Four Rangers were badly injured and three were killed in this bungled part of the operation. Nonetheless, these events led to the setting up of an Interim Advisory Council in Grenada until December 1984, when a 15-member parliament was elected, and democracy returned to the island.

On 3 October 1984, the Department of the Army announced the activation of the 3rd Ranger Battalion, and on 3 February 1986 the 75th Infantry was reorganized into the 2,000-strong 75th Ranger Regiment, with headquarters at Fort Benning, Georgia. The lineage, honours, awards and campaign credits of the Second World War and Korean Ranger units were added to the 75th Ranger Regiment, which had originally drawn its lineage from the 5307th Composite Unit (Provisional). Not since the days of Darby's Ranger Infantry Battalions of the Second World War, had so many Rangers been assembled into a single fighting unit. A new era in Ranger history had begun.

JUST CAUSE

The entire Ranger Regiment participated in Operation 'Just Cause' on 20 December 1989, during which US forces restored democracy to Panama. Rangers spearheaded the action by conducting two important missions. The 1st Battalion, reinforced by C Company, 3rd Battalion, and Regimental Headquarters 'Team Gold', conducted an early morning low-level parachute assault on to Omar Torrijos International Airport and Tucumen Military Airfield, to neutralize the Panamanian Defence Force 2nd Rifle Company, and secure airfields for the arrival of the 82nd Airborne Division. The 2nd and 3rd Ranger Battalions plus Regimental Headquarters 'Team Black', took the airfield at Rio Hato and seized General Manuel Noriega's beach house. Following the successful completion of these assaults, the Rangers conducted follow-on operations in support of Joint Task Force (South) which moved against Panamanian Special Forces Mountain Troops. The Rangers captured 1,014 enemy prisoners of war, and over 18,000 arms of various types, at a cost to themselves of five killed and 42 wounded. Having accomplished their mission, and removed Manuel Noriega and various members of the Panamian Defence Force from power, the Rangers returned home on 7 January 1990.

In 1991, the Rangers participated in Operation 'Desert Storm' with elements of B Company and 1st Platoon, A Company, 1st Battalion, 75th Ranger Regiment, deploying to Saudi Arabia from 12 February to 15 April. Sustaining no casualties, they conducted pin point raids and provided a quick reaction force in co-operation with Allied forces, and contributed significantly to the overall success of the operation.

From 26 August to 21 October 1993, B Company and a Command and Control Element of the 3rd Battalion, 75th Ranger Regiment, took part in 'Operation Restore Hope'. Deployed to Somalia under overall command of Major General William F. Garrison, they assisted United Nations forces in bringing order to a desperately chaotic and starving African nation. The mission of 'Task Force Ranger' was to capture General Mohammed Farah Aidid, the warlord of southern Mogadishu, plus his top lieutenants, and end the guerilla war which hampered efforts to feed the Somali people.

During August and September, the task force conducted six missions into Mogadishu, all of which were a tactical success. They ran these missions both by day and night, and used both helicopters and vehicles to reach their targets. Although Aidid remained free, the cumulative effect of these missions succeeded in limiting his operations.

On 3 October, Task Force Ranger conducted a daylight raid on an enemy stronghold at the Olympic Hotel, deep in militia-held Mogadishu. The Rangers successfully captured some of Aidid's key aides but went to the assistance of a Black Hawk helicopter shot down by an enemy rocket-propelled grenade. They were quickly surrounded by Somali gunmen, but established a defensive positions and laid down suppressive fire to hold the Somalis at bay. Treating their wounded, they worked to free the pilot's body from the wreckage while fighting raged all around them.

Shortly afterwards, a second Black Hawk was downed and overrun by a Somali mob. Despite a

Third Ranger Battalion, C Company 240G gun team provides security while an assault element moves across the street to clear buildings in an urban environment in the Federal Republic of Germany in 1997.
Russ Bryant

Regimental Reconnaissance
Team conducts HALO
operations at 30,000 feet
over the Federal Republic
of Germany. One of the
missions of a HALO team
is to provide surveillance
on a target or objective,
and thereby provide status
reports to headquarters.
Russ Bryant

heroic defence, all the Americans were killed except the pilot, who was taken prisoner. Two defenders of the crash site, Master Sergeant Gary Gordon and Sergeant First Class Randall Shughart, were later awarded the Medal of Honor posthumously.

The quick reaction force of the 2nd Battalion, 14th Infantry, 10th Mountain Division, was dispatched from Mogadishu Airfield to secure the ground evacuation route. As darkness fell, this unit was reinforced by an *ad hoc* task force consisting of two Ranger rifle companies, two Malaysian mechanized companies, a composite platoon from Task Force Ranger, and one Pakistani tank platoon. For three hours they fought a moving gun battle from the gates of the Port to the Olympic Hotel and the Ranger perimeter. The 2-14th was successful in linking up with the Rangers who began withdrawal under fire along a route secured by Pakistani forces.

As dawn broke over the city, the exhausted soldiers rode, marched, and stumbled into the protection of the Pakistani enclave at City Stadium. B Company, 3rd Ranger Battalion, had sustained a total of six men killed on 3 October 1993. For the 2-14th soldiers, the ordeal had lasted over 12 hours, during which they sustained a total of 29 wounded and one killed. Estimates of Somali militia losses were 300 killed and over 700 wounded. Involving six and a half hours of continuous combat, this was the longest sustained fire fight conducted by the US Army Rangers since the Vietnam War.

Rangers have led the way in battle from the era of the flintlock musket to the age of the starlight scope and M 16A2. Whether it be Rogers' Rangers, Vietnam LRPs, Grenada Raiders, or the veterans of Panama or Somalia, they will always have one thing in common – the Ranger Creed. Composed in 1974 by Neil R. Gentry, the command sergeant major of the 1st Battalion, 75th Ranger Regiment, the Creed acknowledges that the Ranger is trained to move 'further, faster, and fight harder' than any other soldier in the world.

Top, at a demonstration for Vietnam Veterans of the 101st Airborne Division at Hunter Army Airfield, Savannah, Georgia, in 1997, a company of 1st Battalion Rangers conduct an airborne assault to secure an objective. After the completion of the mission, the commander announces its success due to a sniper and spotter from A Company, in place over an hour prior to the unit's arrival. They were concealed about 35 yards in front of the veterans.
Russ Bryant

Middle, a 3rd Ranger Battalion squad leader at Fort Pickett, Kentucky, in 1998 deploys his squad into a defensive posture. Note the smoke canisters and weapons sighting systems on the individual weapons system or M-4A1.
Russ Bryant

Bottom, a 2nd Ranger Battalion mortar team uses the M224 60 mm mortar on patrol at Fort Lewis, Washington State, in 1997, and is given a fire mission from the Fire Direction Centre (FDC). The FDC gives the proper distance, range and elevation to the gunners to put deadly accurate fire on any given target.
Russ Bryant

First Ranger Battalion, B Company First Sergeant and squad leader conduct a walk-by inspection of Class A uniforms at Hunter Army Airfield, Savannah, Georgia, before the company commander inspects his men. Note the E-6 squad leader's HALO (High Altitude Low Opening) Badge, Pathfinder Badge and Expert Infantryman's Badge (EIB), which indicates the extensive training that these men receive.
Russ Bryant

Next page, silhouette of a 3rd Ranger Battalion squad leader as he assigns sector fire after assaulting across an objective at Fort Pickett, Kentucky, in 1998.
Russ Bryant

MILITARY
ILLUSTRATED

Military Illustrated is the leading monthly
military history magazine in the English language.
Since its inception, it has built up an unrivalled
reputation among military historians, enthusiasts,
collectors, re-enactors, and military modellers
for authoritative articles, primary research,
rare photographs, and specially commissioned
artwork spanning the entire history of warfare
from ancient to modern – including the most
popular periods such as World Wars Two
and One, Napoleonic Wars, and ancient and
medieval combat.

Copies of the magazine are available on
newstands and in specialist shops or can
be obtained directly from the publisher
on subscription from:

Military Illustrated
45 Willowhayne Avenue
East Preston
West Sussex
BN16 1PL
Great Britain
Tel: 01903 775121

BIBLIOGRAPHY

Primary Sources

Burford, John, *LRRP Team Leader*,
New York, Ivy Books, 1994.

Ericson, Don & John L. Rotundo, *Charlie
Rangers*, New York, Ivy Books, 1989.

Gallion, C. Warren, *Warren Gallion's
Vietnam 1969*, Website , 1999.

James, William Dobein , *A Sketch of the
Life of Brigadier General Francis Marion*,
Charleston, Gould & Riley, 1821.

John *Gorham Papers*, William L.
Clements Library, The University
of Michigan.

Pope, Daniel, 'Oops, the Russians are
coming!', *Behind The Lines, The Journal
of U.S. Military Special Operations*,
Issue #21, May/June 1996.

Russell, J., Jr. (editor), *The History of
the War between the United States and
Great-Britain*, Hartford, Connecticut,
B. & J. Russell, 1816.

Scott, Robert R. (compiler), *The War
of the Rebellion: A Compilation of
the Official Records of the Union and
Confederate Armies, Washington*,
Government Printing Office, 1880-1901.

Thomson, John Lewis, *History of the
War of the United States with Great
Britain in 1812, and of the War with
Mexico*, Philadelphia: J. B. Lippincott
Company, 1887.

Secondary Sources

Bulletin *of the Fort Ticonderoga
Museum, Vol. VI* (January, 1941), No. 1.

Burford, John, *LRRPs in Action –
Combat Troops Number 11*, Carrollton,
Texas, Squadron/Signal Publications,
1994.

Cuneo, John R., 'Factors behind
the Raising of the 80th Foot in America',
Military Collector & Historian, Winter, 1959.

Editors of Time-Life Books, *The Civil War:
Spies, Scouts and Raiders – Irregular
Operations*, Time-Life Books: Alexandria,
Virginia, 1985.

Jackson, Lieut.-Col. H. M.,
Rogers' Rangers, A History, published
by the author, 1953

Katcher, Philip, *The American Provincial
Corps*, Osprey, Men-at-Arms Series, 1973.

Krueger, General Walter, *From Down
Under to Nippon – The Story of Sixth Army
in World War II*, Washington, D.C., 1953.

Lanning, Michael Lee, *Inside the
LRRPs: Rangers in Vietnam*, New York,
Ivy Books, 1988.

Lyles, Kevin, *Europa Militaria Special
No. 3, Vietnam Uniforms in Colour
Photographs*, London, Windrow &
Greene, 1992.

Lyles, Kevin, *US Infantry Vietnam*, Hong
Kong, Concord Publications Co., 1996.

Newark, Tim, Quentin Newark & Dr. J. F.
Borsarello, *The Book of Camouflage*,
London, Brassey's, 1996.

Rogers, Robert J., *Rising Above
Circumstances: The Rogers Family
in Colonial America*, Quebec, Sheltus
& Picard, Inc., 1998.

Rottman, Gordon L., *US Army Rangers
& LRRP Units 1942-87*, London, Osprey
Publishing, 1987.

Stanton, Shelby L., *Rangers at War:
Combat Recon in Vietnam*, New York,
Orion Books, 1992.

RANGER DIRECTORY

Memorials

The Ranger Memorial, Fort Benning, Georgia. Contact the Ranger Memorial Foundation, P.O. Box 53369, Fort Benning, Georgia 31995-3369. Phone: 706-687-0906.

Vietnamese Ranger and American Ranger Advisor Memorial, Arlington National Cemetery, Virginia.

US Army Ranger Antelope Island Memorial, Salt Lake City, Utah.

Vietnam Memorial Wall, Washington, D.C. Pays homage to the 58,000 Americans who gave their lives for their country during the Vietnam War.

'The Moving Wall'. A half scale replica of the Vietnam Veterans Memorial in D.C., this travels around the US, spending about six days at each site.

Trung Son National Memorial Cemetery. Near Con Thien in the DMZ, this harbours the remains of over 10,000 North Vietnamese soldiers and civilians who were killed during supply operations along the Ho Chi Minh Trail.

Vietnamese-American Peace Park. Under construction, this project was begun in 1993 by two veterans, Mike Boehm & Nguyen Ngoc Hung, and is located near Bacgiang, 35 miles from Hanoi.

State of California Vietnam Veterans Memorial. Located in State Capitol grounds at 15th Street and Capitol Avenue, Sacramento. Sculptures represent many sides of the war, with soldiers, nurses, and POWs.

Connecticut Vietnam Veterans Memorials, located in Danbury, Granby, and Plainville. Links are provided for Memorials in New Fairfield.

'The Wall South' is the Pensacola Florida Vietnam Veterans Memorial.

New York Vietnam Veterans Memorials, consist of the Lake Luzerne Memorial, the Westchester County Vietnam Veterans Memorial at Lasdon Park, and the Rensselaer County Vietnam Veterans Memorial.

Virginia's Vietnam War Monument is located in Huntington Park; Newport News, Virginia.

'The North Wall' is the Canadian Vietnam Veterans Memorial, located in Windsor, Ontario.

Australian Vietnam Veterans Memorial is located in Canberra, Australia.

There are many more memorials in virtually every city in the US. Contact local agencies for details.

Associations

Ranger Regiment Association, P O Box 55843, Ft. Benning, GA 31905, U.S.A.

'Sua Sponte' – LRRP-Ranger Association. Contact Steve 'Sour' Crabtree (President Board Member), 225 N. Azurite, Mesa, AZ 85207, USA.

American Infantry Preservation Society (A.I.P.S.) Contact Stuart Beeney (membership secretary), Knowle Cottage, Lower Horsebridge, Hailsham, E. Sussex, BN27 4DL, England. Phone: 01323 843456. Dedicated to the commemoration of the US Infantryman in the Vietnam War.

Vietnam War Historical Society, Contact Paul Hiraldi, 914 Jacaranda Street, Ontario, CA 91762. USA. Phone 909 983-0326

Vietnam Children's Fund. Contributions to the school building project may be sent to: VCF, PO Box 1015, Yonkers, New York 10704-1015, USA.

Websites

75th Ranger Regiment Association:
http://www.75thrangers.org/hq/hq1.htm

Ranger Association Index:
http://www.ranger.org/root/assoc.htm

The Ranger Regiment Association Homepage:
http://www.therangerstore.com/

Ranger Fact Sheet:
www.benning.army.mil/RTB/history2/lrrpmerr.htm

Ranger Links Page:
ranger.org/links/links.htm

Company E (Long Range Patrol),
20th Infantry (Airborne) & Company C (Ranger),
75th Infantry (Airborne) Association Inc.:
http://netsvc.com/ranger/index.html

F Company, 75th Infantry (Airborne):
www.lrrp.com/history.htm

'Sua Sponte' — LRRP-Ranger Association.
Website of E Company, 51st Infantry/
G Company, 75th Infantry (Airborne):
www.paulbunyan.net/users/ssponte/

The LRRP/Rangers of the Vietnam War.
Website of H Company, 75th Infantry (Airborne):
www.geocities.com/Pentagon/5346/

The 4th Infantry Division's Ranger Long Range
Recon Patrol Home Page: This site is devoted to
K Company, 75th Infantry (Airborne) information:
www. 4thdivrangers.com/

LRRP stories & Warren Gallion's Vietnam 1969.
Website for K Company, 75th Infantry (Airborne):
userpages.nkn.net/wgal/frmstory.html

173rd Airborne Brigade Lurps & Rangers.
This site is devoted to N Company,
75th Infantry (Airborne) information:
http://www.75thassoc.org/units/n_75/

Ranger Team 1-6 'Dowd's Dirty Half Dozen':
This site is devoted to:
p.-75th-ranger-team-1-6.com/

Medal of Honor Citations — Vietnam War
1964-1972:
http://www.mishalov.com/Citations.html

INDEX

ACKNOWLEDGEMENTS

The author would like to thank the following, without whose help this study would not have been possible: Terry B. Roderick, president of the 75th Ranger Association; Jim Grimshaw, President of USARA; Mir Bahmanyar, Associate Historian and 2/75 Unit Representative, 75th Ranger Regiment Association; Karl Monger, webmaster, ranger.org; Daniel Pope, Historian, Co. E (LRP) 20th Infantry (Abe) and Co. C (Ranger), 75th Infantry (Abe) Association, Inc.; John L. Rotundo; Don Ericson; Frank Benns; Ralph 'Skip' Resch; Gene Boyd; Hilan Jones; Roy Barley; Bill Cheek; Mike Kentes; Fred Stuckey; Rick Ehrler; Thomas P. Dineen, Jr.; Bob Simpson; Ron Christopher; Ron Bitticks; Lou Bruchey; Ted Yoshimura; Glen McCrary; David Hill; Roger Anderson; Emmett Mulroney; Jim Zwiebel; Larry Flanagan; Tom Reed: Warren Gallion; David Doss; Bob Crawford; Ron Coon; Ron Edwards; John Burford; Bob Gilbert; Peter Mossman; Tom Snow; Robert Dowd Sr.; Rene Chartrand; Alan Thrower; Shelby Stanton; Peter Newark; Russ Bryant; Paul Miraldi; Michael Winey, Curator of Photography, United States Army Military History Institute, Carlisle, Pennsylvania; Ian Carter, Photograph Archivist, Imperial War Museum, London; Felicity Holdom; Andrea Jones and the Bibliographic Services Team, Gloucestershire County Library; Elizabeth Lal, Library Manager, Stow-on-the-Wold Library, Gloucester Library Services; Debbie Shaw, Smalley's Photographic Lab; David Durston; Andrew Pedley, Photographer; special thanks to Ivy Books/Ballantine Books, of New York, for use of extracts from 'Charlie Rangers' by John L. Rotundo and Don Ericson; and grateful thanks to Neil Holdom & Alex Allen for so generously sharing their collection, knowledge, and wisdom regarding the uniforms and equipment of the Vietnam War LRRPs, LRPs, and Rangers.